BLUE DESERT

BLUE DESERT

CHARLES BOWDEN

The University of Arizona Press
Tucson

The University of Arizona Press
© 1986 The Arizona Board of Regents
All rights reserved

www.uapress.arizona.edu

Library of Congress Cataloging-in-Publication Data
Bowden, Charles.
Blue desert.
ISBN 978-0-8165-1081-8 (paper : acid-free paper)—
1. Human ecology—Southwest, New. 2. Human ecology—
United States.
I. Title.
GF504.S685B69   1986
304.2'0979   86-11413

Manufactured in the United States of America on acid-free,
archival-quality paper.

15   14   13   12   11   11   10   9   8   7   6

They soon forgat his works; they waited
  not for his counsel:
But lusted exceedingly in the
  wilderness, and tempted God
  in the desert.
And he gave them their request;
  but sent leanness into their soul.

Psalms 106:13, 14, 15

Coordinates of Blue Desert

1

For three years, I worked at the *Tucson Citizen*, an afternoon daily newspaper, and much of this book comes from that experience. Some of the material appeared in the paper in a different form. A lot of it did not lend itself to the strictures of journalism. It is almost a custom now to mock newspapers as shallow, unfair, and inaccurate. I liked the business. All in all, the *Citizen* was probably the best place I ever worked. I am grateful for the freedom I was given by my bosses.

An earlier version of the chapter on the shell trade appeared in *The Texas Humanist*.

Various drafts of this book have been read by Edward Abbey, Dave Brown, Bill Broyles, Kathleen Dannreuther, Julian Hayden, Lawrence Clark Powell, and Dick Vonier. I want to thank them for their help, kindness, and tolerance. My dog Ben would read none of it and is in no way responsible, legally or morally, for anything in this book. The same goes for the cats, Vincent, Fiddler, and Petunia.

C. B.

Coordinates of Blue Desert

I have lived in the Sonoran Desert since I was a boy and unless I get unlucky, I will die here. My home is a web of dreams. Thousands move here each year under the banners of the New West or the Sunbelt. This is the place where they hope to escape their pasts—the unemployment, the smoggy skies, dirty cities, crush of human numbers. This they cannot do. Instead, they reproduce the world they have fled. I am drawn to the frenzy of this act.

This book proceeds, much the way I do, in a disorderly, relentless fashion. It is fat with contradictions but sounds one steady note: the land.

Imagine you are on a train highballing through the desert night and out the window conflicting scenes flash across your eyes—a glimpse of mountain in the moonlight, a murder barely observed through a motel window—and that these experiences jar against each other as the train thunders toward its destination. This is the way to blue desert.

My world stretches from the New Mexico line across the southern part of Arizona to the Colorado River. It dips south into Mexico and drifts north to the edge of the Colorado Plateau where the hot deserts surrender to the high, cold ground of the central Rocky Mountain West. Here the land always makes promises of aching beauty and the people always fail the land.

This book is about that experience.

It begins at night. The sweet smoke rolls over our bodies as we

1

huddle around the mesquite fire in the December cold. Across the dry river I can see the new jail, a tower with slit windows rising like a sad ghost. Cars stream over the modern bridge and to my back the freeway traffic of Interstate 10 roars. Nearby sits Sentinel Peak where early settlers in Tucson watched for Apaches, and all around us are the stone bones of Indian villages.

The Mexican men ignore the city. We hold tin cups of coffee in our hands and savor the warm smoke. This is one of many vigils for the Virgin of Guadalupe taking place tonight, all because 400 years ago a brown woman who had never lain with a man appeared to an Indian in the Valley of Mexico and gave him roses. The men of Kroeger Lane smoke and laugh while the women busy themselves nearby tending kettles of menudo, stacks of tortillas, and a huge light blue pot of strong coffee. Just down the dirt road, an old lady hosts a shrine to St. Jude in her garden. A block past her, a Mexican woman in her nineties lives alone wrapped in her memories of being a *soldadera* with the *Villistas* during the Revolution. Beyond her is the freeway and then the tower of Santa Cruz church—the twelve-year-old boy by my side goes there to learn how to box.

The city stretches as an endless sea of lights and under the glare live more than a half million people—growing by 25,000 a year as my fellow citizens flee their old American lives for a shot at a new answer, the Sunbelt. All around us are mountains—the Tucsons, the Sierritas, the Santa Ritas, the Rincons, the Santa Catalinas, the Tortolitas.

My hands are cold and I make notes with difficulty. For three years I have traced the life of the boom, sketched little stories for the newspaper. They fall into print as tiny milestones, tiny headstones. As I scribble these dispatches from the current economic miracle of the desert—a bumper crop of subdivisions—the city changes, stretches, takes on new forms, adds 75,000 or 100,000 souls, marries and buries and escapes all the careful strictures of zoning, permits, elections, urban plans. I am in love with the place.

A man disappears from the fire circle, comes back, and adds more mesquite to the blaze. The motel signs wink along the freeway, the aroma of the menudo wafts across our faces.

There are big theories about this sprawl that surrounds me tonight: Republican theories of constructing a new majority, economic theories of a Sunbelt gutting a Rust Belt, car dealer theories of endless growth and prosperity, old guard theories of brown hordes seeping through the fence sixty miles south and Mexicanizing the Republic. The theories are thin gruel. The menudo is rich with the odor of tripe and seasonings. The theories all come from numbers, from sterile offices where anxious, pinched faces ponder paper and issue reports. The menudo comes from the lining of a cow's stomach, two hooves, hominy, spices, and hours at a simmer.

The Mexicans start arguing about the statue of Pancho Villa that takes up a downtown traffic island. The damn thing arrived as a surprise gift from the Mexican government. In Mexico City there is no statue to Villa; he is too frightening a thing for the politicians and bureaucrats to contemplate. He killed people—Mexicans, Americans, Chinamen. But Arizona's Governor, in one of those hands across the border moments, accepted the huge statue of Villa astride his war horse and lusting for the next enemy of the poor. The monument is sited so that Villa stares at the barrios to the south and inexplicably turns his back on City Hall, the County building, the tower of courtrooms.

The Mexicans say the statue is a fraud, a false statement of Villa. Have you looked closely at the statue? they ask me. The horse has no *huevos*. The horse is a mare.

Pancho Villa never rode a mare, they snort.

No, I think, how could he? Men who ride mares do not get statues.

I leave at midnight and file. The vigil is one more scrap for my mosaic of the Sunbelt: file under Happy Note, the persistence of folk culture. Then there are all the things I do not file: the woman who calls me up when I write a story about her fourteen-year-old son who was found as a heap of bones in the desert. What gives you the right to print a story about my son? she asks. The tortured mother who begs me not to put her in the paper when her son, a convicted serial rapist, escapes prison. The cop who pegs the origin of the booming rape rate to the moment "when all the niggers started going down to the University." The businessman who smiles at me as if I were a tot when I question a population explosion in a place with no water and who advises me, "You know you can't build a wall around the place." The wolves endlessly pacing at the zoo and extinct in the desert itself.

I am no good at theories. I cannot say easily words like Progress. I distrust words like Growth. I laugh at the Rotarian ring of Sunbelt. I am tied to the desert and I always live in the city. My Southwest does not fit the plans or reports or newspaper columns. If I have a sense about the Southwest, it is best expressed by a line from Abraham Lincoln, a man who never saw the place or probably gave it much thought:

"Laws change; people die; the land remains."

The morning after the vigil for the Virgin I go downtown and look at Villa's horse. Sure enough the men were right. The thing has no balls.

I am in the boom and I try to catch the roar.

BEASTS

A lion has been seen several times last week.... This would be an excellent opportunity for some of the boys to go out some night and kill him.

Arizona Weekly Star, May 27, 1886

The door is unlocked, the living room clean, antiseptic, and cold. The police have not bothered to seal the crime scene. Images of Christ and the Virgin hang on the walls making promises.

In the next room, the bed is empty. The cops have gone now, carrying the body of the old man flopping in a zippered rubber bag. He lived eighty some years, the priest came every day, and a Mexican housekeeper visited and saw to his needs. Green Valley, a retirement community twenty-five miles south of Tucson, sells peace and quiet. The town barely knows crime.

It happened sometime last night. His face was bashed in. He never made it off his sick bed. Someone swung a baseball bat once, twice, perhaps more. The old man loved baseball and had hung on to his childhood bat decade after decade. He kept it right in his bedroom where he could look at it and remember the sunny days and green grass and good hits. The bedside lamp is crumpled by a blow. And a dried pool of blood mars the cool linoleum floor.

The photographer refuses to enter the room.

I say, "Take a picture, I want the blood."

"They'll never use it," she complains.

"I want it."

Outside cactus wrens scold in the palo verde trees and across the river the Santa Rita Mountains reach with green shoulders into the morning sky.

I catch the priest leaving the rectory and he is old, Irish and gray-headed. A terrible thing, he says, a terrible thing. And then he hurries to the church for Mass.

I call the story in to the rewrite man who says uh huh, uh huh, as the sentences tumble along. The story makes the first edition and runs above the fold—a good murder helps street sales.

The photographer proved right. They never ran the photo.

Bats

THE AIR SCREAMS, rustling movements feather against the skin, squeaks and screeches bounce off the stone walls, and a sweet acrid stench rolls across the room. My mouth chews the darkness like a thick paste.

We stand in feces, hills of feces, and the grey powder slops over our running shoes and buries our ankles. Behind us the light glows through the cave entrance, a slit sixty-five feet high and twenty-four feet wide. Above us the screams continue, the rustling frolic of life. The rock walls feel like cloth to the touch; a wilderness of fungus thrives in the warm room.

We climb. The hills of feces roll like trackless dunes. Our feet sink deeply into the grey powder as we move up toward the ceiling. Here and there a feather: a primary off a turkey vulture; a secondary off a black hawk. There is no explanation for their presence. The odor seems to ebb as our senses adjust to the stench. The dunes toss like waves and in between the dark mounds writhe masses of beetle larvae. Here we find the bones—skulls, femurs, rib cages, and the like.

This is the forbidden place, the dark zone claimed by nightmares. The air can be rich with rabies and people and animals have died from visiting such places. Up high, up near the ceiling, the rustling grows louder and louder. They are disturbed as we march into their world. The eye sees blackness but the skin feels the rustling, the swoosh of something near our brows, our throats, our mouths. We are enveloped in a swirling mass of energy and we keep walking toward the center of this biological bomb.

Something is crawling up our bare legs, across our bellies, down our arms, past our necks and onward into the curious contours of our faces. Mites move up from the dunes of feces and explore us like a new country. When we pause and look up, our eyes peer into a mist, a steady drizzle of urine and feces cascading from the ceiling.

I have no desire to leave. The feces and urine continue to shower down, the mites tickle the surface of my body, the atmosphere tastes like a bad meal and always the air drifting like a thick fog promises the whisper of rabies.

We have come to the charnel house, a bastion of a world in the twilight of its life. The crackling energy swirling in the air around us is dying. And we and our kind are the killers.

This is the bat cave and 25,000 *Tadarida brasiliensis mexicana* wrap us with their anxiety. Night is falling outside the cave. Soon our world will become theirs.

Then they will exit and plunder the canyons, the mesas, the hillsides, the towns, the fields. They will bring back deadly reports of our world, details buried deep in their bones and body chemistry.

The sound tightens now, a shrill spike of screeches and squeaks. The mites scramble across the skin. The larvae writhe like shiny stones at our feet.

We stand inside a brief island of life, a hiding place of our blood kin.

We have known each other a good long while. We would pluck the eye of a live bat, stick it in a wax figure of a dog, put the effigy at a crossroads and hope a lover would come to our bed. We would make an ointment of frankincense, the blood of a lizard, the blood of a bat and treat trachoma. We would carve the image of a bat on the tip of a rhinoceros horn to ward off demons. We would cut the head off a live bat and place it on someone's left arm to cause insomnia. We would crucify live bats, heads downward, always downward and place the result over our doors to fight evil, to protect our sheep, to insure our wakefulness.

We have hated bats. We still hate bats. They own the night and mock our helplessness. Their faces to our eyes look cruel, fierce, ugly.

For thousands of years, they rode through our dreams, they drank our blood, they stood as symbols of a world we were reluctant to enter but a place we lusted for—the black nights, the witches' sabbaths, the magic chants, the scream under a full moon.

This time we have come for them wearing the mask of science. Ronnie Sidner is in her thirties now and she was raised in a tract house along a wooded draw outside Philadelphia. She wanted to become a veterinarian and found her path blocked by a male-dominated profession. She is a small, light-boned woman with red hair but she looks large and angry when she recalls this part of her life.

She decided to go West and wound up a schoolteacher in Parker, Arizona, a small town in the hard ground along the Colorado River where the Mojave and Sonoran deserts rub against each other. She stayed six years and then the emptiness of the American classroom burned her out and left her barren of ambitions. She took a summer course at Northern Arizona University in Flagstaff and the class focused on bats.

Something quickened in her, perhaps the memory of walks along the wooded draw behind her childhood home, the drive to be a veterinarian, or some simple, animal need. She enrolled in the University of Arizona at Tucson and rode to a Master's degree in biology. And she rode bats.

I first met her in the Chiricahua Mountains. She was wearing a t-shirt that proclaimed: I LOVE BATS. By then she was deep into her doctorate, a sprawling, undefined investigation held together solely by bats, thousands and thousands of bats. We talked and then there seemed nothing to do but go to the dark stone room.

I keep thinking it is something about the newspaper business, something about the killings and the people with defeat on their faces that has kindled a bad appetite within me for gore, for ruin and bankruptcy, for bulldozers knocking down giant cactuses so that shopping centers may flourish. But I constantly reject this sense of myself and am angered when others force this black cloak on my shoulders. I like to remember being a boy on that Illinois farm and I am holding a cane pole down by the creek and the fish are jumping. The sun skips off the quiet pools of water and the air comes fresh from Eden. Up by the house the old man and his cronies are drinking beer from quart bottles and marching toward a Saturday afternoon drunk. Below the barn, the Holsteins graze and cool spring water skims across the limestone floor of the milk house. And I am in the sun, and this is what I want and who I am.

I sit at my desk at the paper and stare at the blank wall and when the call comes, and it always comes, I volunteer for the bad deaths, the slaughters called meaningless in our silicon chip society. The ones that do not compute. Because for me, on some level I cannot say, they do compute. I am the one basking in the hot blaze of the Sunbelt who always senses these periodic eclipses when the land goes suddenly dark.

The assistant city editor is standing before my desk with a crooked smile. I can see him just past my boots propped up on my idle typewriter. He wears an Izod shirt. He tosses a police report down and says, "You'll like this one, Captain Death." And I go, I always go, and my entire being picks up and rises. I can sense this eclipse and I want to write it down. The Sunbelt has so much energy, so many slabs being poured, so much land being slain, so much action and I know amidst this frenzy there are these eclipses when the sun goes black and the temperature drops, these little deaths of the blazing white light. And I do not want these moments to go unnoticed. I am certain of this lunatic mission when I flip on the evening news and see the smiling faces or when I read the front page and the headlines chatter about growth, new jobs, booms, and dreams of freeways.

So when I hear of this hole in the earth where bats linger, I must go. Right now, not a moment's delay. There is a huge eclipse of the sun taking place and attention must be paid. I know my job.

The cave is near Clifton and Morenci, two eastern Arizona mining towns at the foot of a wilderness country stretching northward toward Blue River. In the early 1960s, millions of bats lived in the colony. E. Lendell Cockrum, a University of Arizona professor in the Department of Ecology and Evolutionary Biology, tried to tally them once. He made sample counts, multiplied and came out with 50,000,000 bats. Trying to be conservative, he published a figure of 25,000,000.

The big colony once devoured 80,000 pounds of Arizona insects a night. By the late 1960s, there were 25,000 bats and they ate about ninety-eight pounds of insects a night. The devastation of the bat colony came quickly and that fact is what has brought us to the cave. A holocaust has taken place here and I want to visit the place of the great death. Few have noticed this event; fewer cared.

The walk in means miles of wading a stream guarded by light brown canyon walls. As we hike, a zone-tailed hawk explodes from a tree and slashes across the canopy of cottonwoods and sycamores. A red hepatic tanager and his mate watch from a mesquite, the blaze of a vermilion flycatcher spins and twirls off a bare limb. Half-wild steers charge through the brush before us. The water feels warm, the stone bottom slippery under our shoes. Fish dart from our footsteps. Stretches of the stream form still ponds reflecting the high canyon walls and the blue sky.

This is a throwaway canyon in Arizona, a place that in much of the United States would qualify as a national monument, but here in the careless riches of the West's wild land is regarded as simply another slit through the high country, a name on a map that few visit.

The smell hits us like a slap in the face. We look up and there is the huge vaulting door to the cave. We have found the core of the dying.

We pitch our packs under cottonwoods on the canyon's far side and wade back across the stream. Ronnie leads the way and her excitement quickens our steps.

Like us, they are mammals. Their blood is warm and they nurse their young. One out of every five species of mammals is a bat. Forty-five million years before the first beast that looked like a human being walked this earth, bats took to the sky. The early bat jumped from tree to tree after insects and over time the arm became the wing and the air became a new floor for life.

Eight hundred fifty species now swirl across the planet's skin and twenty-four can be found in Arizona. *Tadarida brasiliensis mexicana*, the Mexican free-tail, roams from Texas westward and winters deep in Mexico. This small bat rides on a wingspan of about a foot. The hair runs from dark brown to dark gray. They favor caves—thirteen in Texas, five in Oklahoma and one each in New Mexico, Arizona and Nevada.

These hunters search the desert and sometimes feed as high as

9,200 feet. They can live in colonies of millions, huge masses of bats squeaking, chattering, and crawling across each other. When big colonies once exited from their caves, the sound, according to early observers, thundered like the roar of white water and the dark cloud could be seen for miles. They fly into the night at about thirty-five miles per hour, then accelerate to around sixty. At dawn, they make power dives back into the cave, sometimes brushing eighty miles per hour.

They feed on small moths, ripping the abdomens from them in flight, and may travel forty miles in any direction seeking prey. The young, one per female per year, immediately crawl up the mother hunting the breast. At first, the mother returns several times during the night to nurse and then less frequently. No one is certain if the females find their own young in the huge colonies or nurse the first young bat they encounter. They can live perhaps fifteen years—no one is sure.

Bats remain a mystery in many ways. Science has come to them late in the day. They have been banded and migrations of 1,000 miles recorded. They have been kidnapped and released to test their homing instincts and a return of 328 miles has been observed.

And they have been dying. Oklahoma had 7 million Mexican free-tails and is now down to fewer than 1 million. Carlsbad Caverns had around 9 million and is down to 250,000. And the cave on the creek in the canyon near Clifton and Morenci had its 25 million or perhaps even 50 million and is down to 25,000 or fewer.

There have always been ways for bats to die. In the 1960s, man offered them a new way.

White bones lace across the dark guano like thin wires. The remnants outline a wing that fell from the ceiling. Small skulls peek through the feces, the tiny craniums empty of brains. Ronnie and I keep moving further into the cave. The room stretches 288 feet across, 65 feet high. Up at the peak runs a deep crevice where the bats now live. We have forgotten about the outside world and joined the darkness.

Ronnie picks up a skull and runs her fingers over the white smoothness.

"Oh, skulls," she says, "look at the baby skulls. It's a graveyard."

Bats circle over our heads. They are warming up for the evening flight. At 6:32, they suddenly swoosh out of the cave and stream from the top of the vault. A funnel forms in the center of the canyon and vanishes as the cloud of bats goes north. The flight is over in moments. It is merely the preliminary to the main evening takeoff.

We look back down at the bones, the lacework of bones on the dark guano in the hot cave squeaking with the life of the dwindling colony.

Around the turn of the century, they packed guano out on burros and then loaded it onto trains for fertilizer needs of the West Coast. The haul reportedly earned a profit of $30,000. Later owners of the cave would mine it every five years or so with the last excavation occurring in 1958.

Scientists heard of the cave in the fifties and Cockrum came in 1958. He had been banding bats since the early forties and published books on the mammals of Kansas, Arizona, and the Southwest.

He tried various schemes to catch the bats for banding and finally found a trap that worked. Bats present special problems. Rabies shots are often necessary because the caves form a perfect medium for the virus. Caged animals placed beneath the colonies have died from the disease although no bat could possibly have reached through the mesh containers to bite them.

Banding offered its own woes. The bats chew off bands within six weeks and less than one tenth of one percent of the banded bats were ever recovered.

Cockrum reveled in the bat colony at its height—one estimate made in June 1964 pegged the population at 50 to 100 million bats. By June 1969 the census estimate was 30,000.

Cockrum remembers the cave in the good times when the first evening flight required thirty minutes and the main event began at dusk and roared on until midnight.

"At dawn," he laughs, "we'd be sitting there banding these god-damn bats and you could hear the flutter of the bats as they came in on a power dive."

Inside the cave, the ceiling and walls were covered, the crevice could not even be seen under the mass of bats, and the animals hung far down the sides. Cockrum could just reach up and pluck them.

Cockrum is a hearty man now in his sixties. He sits in his university office and drifts easily back to the bat cave of the sixties.

"It was a constant, loud, intensive noise," he says, "a constant stream of bats flying. A constant rain of mites as well as urine and guano. After you'd been in there ten minutes, you could feel things crawling on your skin and you'd go out and see these dots crawling up your arms."

But what he remembers best is the seething mass of beetle larvae on the cave floor.

"This was fresh guano," he says. "This surface was almost a sea of larvae and any bat that died or baby that fell to the floor was immediately devoured. Within thirty minutes you'd have a clean skeleton."

Outside green blazes off the trees and the stream slides like a brown skin over the rocks. Light ebbs from the canyon. We climb down from the dunes of guano, slip off the rock shelves to the cave opening. The night begins to come down.

Ronnie holds a feather and the delicate finger bone of a bat. And then it begins.

"Oh, my God," she says. "Oh, look at them all. This is great!"

Urine and feces rain down on us. We look up and we cannot look away. Bats storm across the top of the vault, a torrent of wings and squeaks. They streak to the canyon center and swirl and then funnel off. This is the major flight. The free-tails give a faint echo of the thunder of twenty years ago when perhaps 100 million tiny mammals squealed from the room in the rock wall and took to the night sky, an army of hearts, lungs, and fangs ranging out twenty, thirty, forty miles, beasts ripping the soft abdomens from moths, feasting in the dark hours.

A crescent moon hangs and the bats become fine lines etching the glowing face. In four minutes it is over. A flight that once took hours is now 240 seconds. The cave falls silent.

They are gone.

When Cockrum finished his banding, 88,176 bats had been tagged. From this he plotted the colony's migration route from Arizona to Sonora and Sinaloa in Mexico. This helped him understand the dying.

When the bodies were examined back in the laboratory, the scientists found dieldrin, toxaphene, and DDT. The colony kept shrinking and Cockrum began to understand why. He had already noticed that bats had deserted Tucson. Once they had roosted in the old buildings of the university campus and were a common sight under the street lights. Then with the massive use of household pesticides they vanished.

He began tracking DDT sales in Arizona. Five hundred and forty thousand pounds were sold in 1965, and by 1966 the quantity had reached 1.07 million pounds. In 1967, 2.52 million pounds were poured onto the land. The agricultural district of the Gila Valley lies within easy reach of the bat cave and they fed heavily there.

That might be part of the answer.

When the United States ended the use of DDT in the late sixties, the colony did not repopulate. Below the border, the use of DDT continued, as it does to this day.

The bats acted as sensors for a world man created but ignored. They roamed the global skin where the insects fly and swallowed the parts per million and per billion that human beings measured and monitored. These chemicals were concentrated in the mother's milk and the young suckled lustily.

Cockrum thinks the tradeoff was reasonable. He likes bats and hates the idea of man causing the extinction of any creature. But, he hastens to add, he has worked in the Third World.

He puts it this way: would you rather die of a tropical disease in your twenties or perish in your sixties because of toxic chemicals? But of course, no one polls the bats on their views.

They simply die, humans live, the crops grow. It is part of this time in this century.

The dying goes like this. The young drink the milk laced with pesticides, the pesticides attack their central nervous systems. The small animals start to shake, then motor skills decline. Eventually the feet clinging to the mother or to the ceiling let go. They fall. The mass of beetle larvae move in. In thirty minutes the bones are clean, a fine wire of calcium across the dark guano in the warm cave.

The scream sounds faraway at first, then nearer. We walk out the mouth of the cave. The howling continues, a screech, a long winding yowl as the cry of a big cat shreds the night stillness. We pan with the flashlight.

Twenty feet away two green eyes glow. We move toward the eyes, move instinctively and without hesitation. The cat bounds into the brush and is gone. We crash down the hillside through the thicket of mesquite and hackberry. The stream cools our legs. Bats skim the water sipping drinks. Now outside the warmth of the cave, the mites flee our bodies.

We eat dinner, have a drink of whiskey, and throw our bags down on the ground. Rocks fall from the nearby cliffs as bighorn sheep hop from ledge to ledge.

We are very excited by the memory of the bats brushing against our faces, by the roar of the evening flight, by the green glow of the mountain lion's eyes. Around midnight, the screaming returns. The cat moves around our camp howling. Scientists speculate that this behavior is territoriality, that the lion is staking out its share of the earth. We listen to the screams in the warm night and we do not wonder at what they mean. They say this is my ground, my place.

The sound pierces our half-sleep and then after fifteen or twenty minutes drifts down the canyon. Quiet returns and the screams persist only in our dreams.

Bats squeak overhead as they begin to hunt the poisoned skies and fields. They have few friends in the world of man. They are the demons of our dreams and their slow chemical death is not a matter of concern for many.

We lie under a roof of stars, wings rustling above our faces.

The lion does not return.

He wears camouflage clothing, dabs his face with dark ointment to disguise the flesh, and moves slowly and quietly across the high grassland of northern Arizona. He does this for days, looking for his chance. When we were boys, we hunted together but now that has ended for me. A few years ago I sold him my Parker double, a kind of sad admission that we would never kill together again. I drifted off into hiking, bird-watching, nature books and joined all the bitter organizations that wail about wildlife and wild ground. We do not speak of these matters because we want to preserve a friendship that means more than all the land.

He turned to archery, for the challenge he explained. And now he creeps with his bow and arrows across the grassland. There are many antelope but they see him too soon and he can never get quite close enough. With his bow, he must be within forty yards, he absolutely must.

Finally, his luck changes, the arrow flies true, and the animal falls. Dusk is coming on. He hurriedly guts the carcass, his fingers fumbling with the sticky, warm entrails. They steam in the cool air. He uses a small pocket knife, a point of pride with him. He despises those who strap huge Bowie knives to their hips. He worships craft and always has the appropriate tool.

He is a big man but does not relish the idea of stumbling for miles in the darkness with his bow and arrows and the body of an antelope. He finds a tree, and hangs the animal.

Getting out takes much longer than he had counted on—the way is not plain in the blackness.

The next day he returns for his trophy. There is very little left. The shoulder and haunches and chest cavity and hide are either gone or in ruins. Much of the head is the same. All he can salvage are the twin black pronghorns. They will have to do.

A lion came in the night. And the lion fed at the man's kill. The man is not angry. He does not explain. Of course, we both know why. We were boys together.

Antelope

THE MEN STAND ON THE RUNWAY and talk of Nam, Beirut, and Grenada and wonder about the possibilities of Central America. Two fixed-wing aircraft and three choppers wait on the cool cement this morning. The men are pilots and they savor war news—old wars, recent wars, future wars. Some of the men are in the Air Force and some are now out but the taste of action, the chance to be there, to be where it is really happening, tugs at them. They believe in American might and they are wounded by each American humiliation. Iran? Oh yes, Iran, they say. That must not happen again.

The tiny runway lies a few miles out of Ajo, a dying Arizona copper town about fifty miles north of the Mexican line. The slabs were poured in World War II to train pilots for Europe and Asia. When that war fell away, the installation went to ruin. Weeds peek now between the cracks in the concrete. The old officers' quarters just to the east has become a country club for the small community's few copper executives.

I lie on the runway and listen to the talk. I have never been in any army or any war but I am not immune to these feelings. The Air Force machines whip up a martial ardor in the men, military and civilian alike. Words stenciled across the chopper act as cue cards:

EXIT RELEASE
PULL SLIDE
BACK ASST.

21

OPERATING LIMITS
DANGER

We are on a set and the set makes us all actors.

Off to the west, on Childs Mountain, a new military outpost pokes up against the horizon. Here millions of dollars of computers, radio equipment, and high-tech witchcraft monitors all the firing on the gunnery range up to the north and west. There is talk of lasers teasing the targets, of drones being towed like cows for practice shooting. Out there the desert is littered with brass and people sneak in to salvage it. Sometimes they get blown up. Sometimes they die of thirst.

We wait to go into that shooting gallery. The day is scheduled to be a cold day—one in which the Air Force will refrain from clotting the sky with hot rounds.

We will not trigger cannons. We prefer nets. And we don't stalk the enemies of the state but pursue a more slippery prey, a life force 10 to 25 million years old.

They have always been Americans. All the fossils and all the living forms on earth come from North America. Once great herds stretched from southern Canada down into Mexico. The subspecies roaming west of Ajo (*Antilocapra americana sonoriensis*) was identified only in 1945, based on an adult female skin and two skulls. The key specimen was killed December 11, 1932. From these bones Americans learned of another American.

We barely know our quarry. We do not know how many there are. We do not know where they go. We do not know how they organize themselves. We do not even know if they drink water. And we cannot imagine what they think.

They are commonly called Sonoran pronghorn. They occupy a small patch of southwestern Arizona and northwestern Sonora. Maybe three or four hundred survive on the surface of the earth, perhaps seventy-five to one hundred, we hope, romp on the American side of the fence. Once they roamed across the Colorado River deep into California and for more than one hundred miles east of Ajo to the edges of Tucson and Phoenix. The ways of man and man's beasts have driven them deep into the dry heat of the desert and here they linger, an echo of a world largely slaughtered long ago.

Mexico has not permitted a legal hunt since 1922 but this law is sometimes winked at. Twenty years ago, four heads from Mexico were seized in a Tucson taxidermy shop. Today, in Sonora, the killing continues disguised with weird government permits and thick bundles of cash slid under the table. In the world of trophy hunting, there are always a few sports who go off the rails and become strange Noahs filling their death ships with one of each species.

On the American side, the antelope now roam over about 2.5 million acres. This is the place where moisture is a dream. At Ajo, the average annual rainfall is 9.1 inches. One hundred and thirty miles to the west, at Yuma, 3.38 inches. And some years it forgets to rain.

The pronghorn blend so well into this minimal landscape that they are almost invisible. I have spoken to game officials who patrol this turf and who have gone for weeks and weeks without sighting one. A recent survey turned up only thirteen in three days of flying.

They survive here because the military needs a place to train for war and this kind of work keeps just about everyone else out—the poachers, the cattle, the hurly-burly of twentieth century ways and means. The land in the military gunsights is part of the Cabeza Prieta National Wildlife Refuge plus the Luke-Williams Gunnery range. Naturally, the Air Force did not originally consider whether rare antelope bounced along on their playing field—or anything else for that matter. But now that the subspecies has been brought to their attention, they are willing to make a good show of it. Luke is bucking to win the Air Force conservation award and tending to endangered antelope looks like a good way.

So they've loaned pilots and aircraft for this hunt. Along with personnel from the U.S. Fish and Wildlife Service and the Arizona Game and Fish Department, the Air Force men will join in an effort to capture, examine, and radio collar at least five antelope. It is hoped that something will be learned that will help pull the small bands back from the abyss of extinction.

At 7 A.M. the two planes take off to scout up some antelope. The choppers and the bulk of us wait around the runway for the call, a wait that could go on and on and on. The hunt has all sorts of little quirks: the antelope cannot be pursued if the air temperature exceeds 80 degrees because they might die from heat stress; they cannot be held captive for more than five minutes for the same reason.

Because we are so ignorant of the antelopes' habits, they cannot be baited into a trap—we have no idea what they like to eat. A new technique, firing a net from a gun powered by a .308 cartridge, has come into recent vogue (no wildlife has yet perished by this method) and this is the weapon of choice this morning.

While the antelope are rare, the bureaucratic agreement on this old runway is even rarer. For several years, the various agencies have haggled over details, money, and tactics. It is a wonder the antelope managed to survive long enough to be chased by helicopters and manhandled by human beings.

One federal official has flown in from Albuquerque, several state experts have come from Phoenix and a small herd of television and print reporters have journeyed from Tucson. None of us came here with terribly clean hands.

The Air Force rules lay down all kinds of restrictions out in the desert Refuge: no plane should normally fly below 3000 feet or ever below 500 feet. I've seen them 100 feet off the ground and one pilot boasted to a friend of mine that he cracked the sound barrier 25 feet from the ground. There are areas where no firing should take place, like waterholes. I've found spent rockets lying around waterholes favored by bighorn sheep. But then, we're hardly likely to recruit men good at flying fighter planes who tend to obey rules. Anyway, the antelope seem to adjust to the jets—they've been sighted feeding with aircraft at 500 feet and have not even raised their heads.

The people from the state Game and Fish Department have a checkered past with antelope—one of the great failures of a general wildlife revival in the state. Antelope can't seem to master jumping fences and as the state goes to more barbed wire and little ranchette estates, remaining sanctuaries for the species are disappearing. The Department responds by haggling a little here and there and periodically shooting coyotes from airplanes to cut down predation of the fawn crop.

The U.S. Fish and Wildlife people have a few bad moments to live with too. As lackeys of the state's cattle interests they almost single-handedly exterminated the wolf (last den with pups found in 1943 and slaughtered) and grizzly bear (last sighted in 1936).

I myself have become almost a functionary for the Air Force in this antelope business, merrily cranking out newspaper stories lauding their efforts in the hope they will accept the delusion and make a major effort to safeguard the beasts.

Meanwhile the antelope have been run over by cars on the highway, poached here and there, drowned in irrigation ditches. And survived. So here we are armed with big machines and science to lend them a helping hand.

At 9 A.M. the scouts call in that antelope have been sighted and we all race for our choppers like Green Berets. We cross the black mountains and cruise the creosote flats and within twenty minutes the band is found. Nine antelope romp along at fifty miles an hour. Two choppers stay one hundred feet off the desert floor and the capture chopper drops down to about eight feet.

The machine dogs the animals and they wheel and turn and charge and spin, trying to shake the strange predator. One man hangs out the open door clutching the gun. After three minutes of harassing the band to wear them out, the man fires and an antelope goes down trapped in the maze of an orange net. All three craft land and we race toward our quarry.

Huge spikes drink the beast's blood, a thermometer is rammed up its ass and a white radio collar snapped on the neck. The antelope is blindfolded to calm it and this spares us the wild look in its eyes. The animal writhes and the body temperature, normally 98 or 99, jumps to 104. We all jockey in and touch. We cannot resist.

There are four or five billion of us, a couple of dozen of them. Everyone must touch.

For years there has been speculation that the pronghorn are mute. They are not.

A deep rattling moan escapes the animal and the warm desert air suddenly chills. No one can mistake the message of the sound, the grieving powering it.

A kind of collision between cultures has taken place. Huge machines that fly at eighty miles per hour and drink more than seventy gallons an hour have snared an organism that has raced at fifty miles per hour for millions of years.

The sound keeps coming and coming. We have violated some deep important thing and we cannot doubt this fact.

The man was stopped on the highway, a flat tire he says, and two guys pulled up. He whipped out his .9 mm pistol and nothing happened. But it made all the difference he wants me to know. He travels the lonely roads of the Southwest a lot. He's a salesman, and he goes armed. He stands there in a white shirt and tie grimly recounting his adventures out there with a shoeshine, a smile, and a fist full of deadly force. His belly looks like pudding.

We are in a gun shop that specializes in semi-automatic pistols, riot guns, and those machine guns that have been altered (at least for the moment) so that they cannot be operated fully automatic. There is nothing in this store that would serve to hunt wild animals. But they are fine tools for shooting targets or people. This causes such weapons to be denounced by some but I do not share this indignation.

The guns are beautiful, all black and blue metal or chrome, cool to the touch, perfectly machined. I love them on sight. The owner stands there with two Colt .45s, one holstered under each arm. He wears a white t-shirt and an expression that says, "Try me."

I ask him if he has ever been robbed.

"Never successfully," he replies, smiling.

Tortoises

I ONCE KNEW a woman who had a pet tortoise named Fluffy and I think of this fact as I face the action.

The blue air hangs over the room of clacking machines as people pack this casino hugging the banks of the Colorado River and wearily pull the levers on the slots.

I am hungry. I check my backpack with the doorman and rub my fingers across the stubble of my beard. The people are very intent and do not look up or around or at one another. Laughlin, Nevada, strings a half dozen casinos along the tame stream and is only a minute by boat from the Arizona shore. Outside the parking lots are packed with campers, trucks, and vans and every machine has a toy poodle yapping at the window. This is a blue collar Las Vegas.

I want bacon and eggs, but I hesitate on the floor of the casino. The players are men in caps and t-shirts, fat-hipped women in polyester stretch pants, retired folks plunging with dimes and quarters. I am pretty much dirty clothes, clumps of greasy hair, and hung-over eyes. Last night I slept in the hills overlooking the valley. Cottontails grazed around my head and hopped along the sides of my sleeping bag. All night the casino signs splashed color and form into the night sky and then at first light, lines of herons and ducks and geese slowly winged down the ribbon of river to the feeding grounds. In this big room of smoke, booze, and slots, sunrise and sunset count for nothing.

Clocks are kept from sight, the pit blocks all views of the outside and the women peddling drinks to the players, God! Those women in black net stockings, thrusting breasts, fresh young faces, and ancient eyes. Well, the women strut through the blue air denying that time or age or bills or tomorrow exists or matters. I love the women and what they are doing for us all. Just savor them, I tell myself, don't speak to them, don't go home with them, just brush them with your eyes. In here, they are the promise of flesh and fun and smiles and I do not want to know about the two kids, the old man that skidaddled, the small trailer where every time you turn around you bump into yourself.

I finally cross the casino floor and walk into the restaurant, a barren that is here and there dotted with tired people pumping coffee and reading the sports pages. I sit down, swallow a couple of cups and start nibbling at the pile of scientific papers I carry. I have come here to listen to experts consider the plight of the desert tortoise and the experts have gathered here from the universities, from the Bureau of Land Management, from the fish and game departments, from all the small offices with gray desks and steady checks, because, hell, why not meet in a casino town?

The desert tortoise itself (*Gopherus agassizii*) has skipped this occasion. In the bright lights and big cities of the Sunbelt this small reptile is no big deal. Loving a desert tortoise is a little bit like bonding with a pet rock—scholars estimate that the beast spends 94.9 percent of its time in dormancy, which means just lying there in its burrow. Today they are being wiped out in the desert, and in Sunbelt cities survive mainly as pets and captives (at least twenty thousand in California and thousands in Tucson and Phoenix). Once upon a time they averaged from ten or twenty up to several hundred per square mile. But this is a new time and a new west.

I thumb through this leviathan study, an 838-page draft report being considered by the Desert Tortoise Council, the cabal of experts zeroing in on this casino for a conference. I discover that *Gopherus agassizii* runs six to fourteen inches, tops the scale at maybe ten pounds and hardly pesters anyone. They endure their slow lives for 50 to 100 years, and I am briefly bewitched by the notion that somewhere out there lumber Methuselah tortoises that have seen the whole western movie, all three reels, from Wyatt Earp to Palm Springs.

The eggs and bacon finally arrive and I devour them. This is a nickel-and-dime trip where I figure on skipping room rent by flopping in the desert, jotting notes during all the weighty sessions of tortoise papers, and hopefully, scribbling a story that will pay the rent.

The tortoise looks to be a perfect foil for a quick hit: they are the innocents, the benign nothings who do not attack cattle, sheep, or hikers, the little rascals who pack no venom and fire up all the fantasies of nature that people relish. Scientists tag them as an indicator species, meaning one that suggests the health of the ecosystem as a whole. Almost stationary in their habits, long-lived, low in reproduction rate and quiet, they function as witnesses to the way human beings in the Southwest treat the land and the forms of life woven into the land.

In short, tortoises have a high potential to evoke human guilt. Box office.

I have been counseled at length by a friend who for decades has flourished as a free-lance writer of nature stories. He warned me to avoid all colorful references to the casino ("none of those clinking ice cubes in glasses of whiskey," he fumed) and play it straight and be rich in technical information. This is good advice that I find hard to follow. I have yet to meet the casino that cannot seduce me. The pits are so full of human greed and human hope and always there are those little touches—the men in the glass room packing sacks of money and wearing smocks that have no pockets—that make me glad to be a human being. There are few places as honest as the rampant fraud and fantasy of a casino. Here we let down our hair, our pants, our everything and confess to all our secret hungers.

The women working the place are a problem also, busting out of their britches, bending down to pour coffee and slapping my face with deep cleavage. I can think of few things more pleasurable than to sleep on the desert, watch the rabbits bounce around and then at dawn walk into a casino where time has stopped and everything always promises to be juicy.

I pay the bill and move up the stairs to the meeting rooms where plump, contented tortoise experts gather over coffee and doughnuts. I strike up conversations with perfect strangers who are all friendly in this bastion of tortoise love. An elderly couple tells me of their son who is in the grocery business and has a kind of tortoise preserve at his home with eighteen of the beasts thriving on the wilted lettuce he brings home each night. A lady from Phoenix brags on her pet male who taps the patio doors when he wants in the house. The registration table for the conference is a gold mine of tortoise pendants, pens, pins, t-shirts, key chains, wind chimes.

Everyone seems satisfied after an evening of frolicking over steak dinners, trying their luck at blackjack, having a spin in this dab of sin—all at government expense. Finally, the session comes to order and I hunch in my chair busy noting the hard facts of *Gopherus* scholarship.

Being a desert tortoise may not constitute a full-time job. A calendar of the tortoise year, based on a daily time budget (DTB) and annual time budget (ATB), is not full of big events. The animals emerge from their holes in late March to late July when the days begin to be warm. At first, basking (tortoise sunbathing) takes up about 19 percent of the DTB, a figure which declines as the season advances, and only kills 1.5 percent of the ATB. Once out and about tortoises turn to foraging (1.5 percent ATB) and love-making (0.08 percent ATB). Even during the friskiest part of the summer season they go dormant 33 percent of the time.

Tortoises spend only three to six months a year actively feeding and moving, and even during this frisky period they devote most of their hours to snoozing in their burrows. Basically, *Gopherus agassizii* is not a Type A personality and this wonderful calm has prevented tortoise scholars from glimpsing much action.

A few tidbits have been gleaned. When picked up and alarmed they are liable to piss all over people. When two male tortoises meet, they bob their heads and often ram each other—the loser being toppled onto his back and left to die in the heat if he cannot right himself. When sprinting they can cover about six yards in a minute but they hardly ever move far from their burrows unless maddened by thirst.

They have very little to say. When disturbed or when mating, they sometimes hiss, grunt, and make pops and poinks. I hesitate in my note-taking and contemplate the ring of a hearty tortoise poink. Dominant males seem to pack a potent punch when they defecate and have been known to send the rest of the boys scurrying from a burrow with one mighty dump.

Sex occurs to a tortoise after reaching the age of fifteen or twenty and the first date begins with the male bobbing his head and then nipping the female a few times on the shell before mounting her. Tortoise women maintain an air of calm and sometimes keep right on eating during copulation. Eggs are laid, buried, and after 100 days, hatch. The young tortoise must face five years of desert life with a soft shell.

Generally, tortoises are homebodies and spend their lives within a few hundred yards of their burrows, wandering off mainly for a little dining, basking, or love-making. Specimens tagged during a study in the late thirties and early forties were found in the same area by scientists in the eighties. They chow down on green herbs, leaves, and blossoms of annuals, succulents, grasses, and cacti.

The papers come one after another and they stand in contrast to the sea of peace that constitutes normal tortoise life. Outside the casino walls in the desert we cannot see well (the meeting room, naturally, has no windows), out there it is holocaust time for tortoises. I look around at conference attendants and see a lot of grim faces.

People, it seems, have been wreaking havoc on tortoises for a long time—they were sold as dog food in Los Angeles during the 1890s—and from this fact has sprung the modern tortoise industry. We shoot them just for the hell of it, hack them to pieces, drive over them with cars, collapse their burrows with off-road vehicles, stomp them to death with our livestock, and starve them to death by running cattle and sheep on their range—beasts which devour all the forage tortoises crave.

Until the 1970s, nobody much cared. Then something new happened—all those federal laws about endangered species and all those new agency mandates demanding environmental impact statements. I take a closer look at the faces in the room and realize I am sitting with the new servants of the desert tortoise. Hacks from the BLM who suddenly must kowtow to a damn reptile because their beloved steers are destroying it. Biologists from game and fish departments who thought they would spend their days keeping tab on deer and antelope and bighorns and elk who now are here fat with statistics about tortoises and management plans for them.

I no longer like the room. I once had a professor who patiently explained to me that I never could stomach any cause once it had become successful. Well, there must be worse sins. I have heartily supported every law, executive order, and petition to salvage the dwindling biological wealth of the earth. But now I see what happens to every decent impulse in my society: they become that ugly thing, government.

I get up and wander out of the meeting. Downstairs time has passed, but mercifully everything has remained the same. I sidle up to the long bar which stares out at the river and sip whiskey as the afternoon sinks toward evening. Others at the bar amuse themselves with electronic poker games and there is an air of deadly serious sport about the place.

The hills bordering the valley bear the traces of Indian trails where tribes of the Colorado once raced north and south for hundreds and hundreds of miles exporting war, magic, and a few hard goods. The ground cover is scant and low and this is not the kind of country most Americans call beautiful. They storm across it in their machines from Phoenix, Tucson, Los Angeles, and more distant parts of the Republic so they, like their fathers before them, can gather at the river. And once here they drink, gamble and feed.

At my back, hunkered over the crap tables, poker tables, and slots, are my fellow citizens hailing from most states in the Union. And none of them are likely to waste much time pondering the plight of a desert tortoise. The couples, ma and pa, tend to wear matching caps and windbreakers. In the gift shop, there is practically nothing to read for sale. The casino seems dedicated to low-level aerobics and no slackers are allowed to pull back and pursue thick books or falter from doing their reps with the slot machines. No pain, no gain.

Denouncing this place would be like coming out against the tooth fairy.

I join the line for the casino cheap feed, a chicken dinner (all you can eat) for a few bucks. Three Indians sit down at my table. Their faces are brown, blank, and immobile. We chomp on the fried birds and slowly words drone from their mouths. They are Navajos working on a stretch of nearby railroad track and they find the casino curious and the food a great bargain. I arrived in the Southwest in 1957 and according to the best reports, my tablemates seized some local turf in the fifteenth century. But we seem to have wound up in the same situation. We ogle the girls, speculate on the thrill of guzzling a few drinks, and say the casino is a real pleasant puzzler.

The Southwest is a place where almost everyone slips their moorings and just drifts. The cities and towns are ugly, the populace footloose, the crime frequent, the marriages disasters, the plans pathetic gestures, the air electric with promise. There is so much space and so much ground that no one can for a single moment doubt the basic American dream that it is possible to make something worthwhile of life. Everything a desert tortoise is—calm, a homebody, long-lived, patient, quiet—the people of the Southwest are not. We don't stay in our burrows much anymore or limit our motion to the cycle of the sun. Just across the road from the casino, a huge powerplant belches smoke into the sky. The facility burns coal mined on Black Mesa in the Navajo and Hopi country of northern Arizona, coal that is piped as a slurry the 278 miles to Laughlin. The electricity generated here is then flashed outward to blaze in the lights of Southern California. Such grids of energy and rivers of energy-flows are the stuff of life in the Southwest and they do not produce a state of mind that cottons to the issue of endangered species. It is not that we are too busy building the empire to tend to details but simply that we are too busy running to ever look back at the ghosts trailing behind us or down at the ground where the writhing beasts shudder with their last convulsion of life. We haven't got time for this nature stuff. We were born to drive, not park.

I walk down the road to a store and buy a pint of whiskey, reclaim my backpack from the doorman, and head back into the hills for another night of stargazing. I lie amid the creosote with my head next to an Ajo lily and study tortoise papers under the flicker of my candle lantern. The documents are grim stuff with the reptile all but gone from the Mojave, being mowed down in Nevada and Utah, still legal game in Arizona. I pour my Sierra cup full of whiskey, blow out the light and witness a falling star.

When I was a kid I once stopped off in Goldfield, Nevada, a failed mining town that boomed around the turn of the century and since has whimpered along with a few cranks and loners lodging in the abandoned houses. The big hotel downtown had been shut for decades and I peered through the windows eyeing the tables all set with linen and silver and wondering if I could make off with some booty. The old man wanted a drink and we walked up the street and found a saloon. The barkeep was a grizzled prospector type with long, gray beard and fat, red nose. His name was Silver Dollar Kirby and his place boasted a plank on two saw horses for the bar and a couple of open bottles and glasses for his stock. My father pumped down a few shots and marveled at a place so free of expensive licenses and gruesome regulations that a fellow like Kirby could open for business with ten dollars worth of assets.

There is not much difference between the proud new Sunbelt cities and the old mining camps. They are both temporary Woodstocks of wanderers hell-bent on plundering. They will exhaust the place and then move on. I should say: we will exhaust the place and then move on. For my body may be sprawled in the desert tonight but a part of me is always seduced by the bright lights of the casino. All over the region I see my handiwork: the ghost towns, the mine scars, the butchered grazing tracts, the dull cities, the highways full of traffic racing to get nowhere, the crap tables, the dammed and maimed rivers. We have taken our main chance and the results only look good on the Dow Jones.

The night slips away and at gray light I march once again on the casino. A man stands outside his van shaving in the rearview mirror. He looks fresh and ready for the long odds offered by the slots. The restaurant is empty and I sit down and administer black coffee when a man joins me. He recognizes me from the conference—a fellow student of tortoise matters.

He is in his mid-thirties, fit and tanned and his beard is neatly trimmed. He works for a national wildlife organization and moves around the Southwest lobbying for this species and that. For him the casino is Babylon and he has spent his time, when not absorbing the scientific papers, sequestered in his room watching athletic events on cable television.

He is a man with a mission. Put simply, his organization is going to file suit against the federal government to make them obey their own laws about endangered species and spring to the defense of the tortoise. Since the reptiles can hardly cope with anything human beings or their livestock like to do, this means locking up big chunks of the Southwest to make them secure for tortoises. The tortoise in this cunning scenario becomes a wonderful tool that will smite many foes. The arrogant ranchers can be felled by the tortoises, the obscene power companies can be toppled, the crazed off-road vehicle freaks and all the minions of industrial life that are sacking the deserts can be chastened, banned, and outlawed.

I appreciate the elegance of the plan. Soon we move past such political stratagems and he begins to remember what got him into this wildlife business, this new religion of the mid- and late-twentieth century that seeks to stop the clock and perhaps wind it backwards to a time when the land was relatively unpeopled and the beasts held sway.

He worked for the National Park Service and saw Alaska, the Rockies, a lot of great country. He wound up in Yellowstone and grew interested in grizzly bears. During one management plan, the local dump was off limits and the bears feasted at the dump. He snuck in with another employee and sat high up on a hill. In the twilight he saw these dark blobs gliding over the grass toward the garbage and suddenly realized he was seeing bears, grizzly bears, the lords of all creation on the North American continent.

He stalls here in his retelling of that evening and searches for the right words, the right expressions. Behind us we can hear the early morning gamblers whacking away at the handles of the slots. But he is in Yellowstone on that hillside and his eyes have that thousand-yard stare.

The grass, the grass had this quality, this color, and the bears, the bears were big, wild and free and he was witnessing them. That is all he can say.

His bosses found out that he had broken the rules and he was promptly fired. That was okay. He had that memory of one evening and now he is in Laughlin, Nevada, representing the interests of desert tortoises and it is all the same thing to him.

I sip my coffee and mumble agreement. Actually, I am moved. I understand what he means. I sense myself on the same hillside. And I cannot explain it either.

The conference continues with a life of its own. I keep reading scientific papers and gorging myself on tortoise numbers. From time to time, I retreat to the bar and drink whiskey, one eye peeled for displays by the cocktail waitresses. I look out at the river and watch the powerboats race past and feel the burn of the booze sliding down my gullet.

The bears come back often, big forms of fur moving across the grass in the twilight. And the tortoises visit me also, hard cases snoring away a century, only to be periodically crushed, stolen, hacked, and shot by my kind.

The cocktail waitress brings me another drink—this time a scotch. I feel expansive. She has great legs, long firm stems sketched by the black net stockings. I want the river, the bear, the tortoise, and those legs.

I walk out the door and across the parking lot. The air hums with sound from the generators rumbling in all the campers, vans and mobile homes. The booze feels wonderfully warm in my gut and twilight slips down.

A line of geese V's up the river and I crane my neck to enjoy the sight. In the windows of the campers I can see the glow of the television screens.

They raise beef. The hands have a finger tip missing here or there,
the necks are creased, the shirts all snaps, boots real leather, levis
faded. We sit around the cool formica table in the cafe and talk ranch
talk, Mogollon Rim ranch talk.

This is lion country and the big cats eat calves, the ranchers hunt
and kill the big cats and over the decades this dance of death had
wrapped them together with hoops of myth. The ranchers hate lions
and base their sense of self on lions.

One rancher tells how once he found two lions copulating, a
moment normally denied even the most ardent student of the secre-
tive cats. The biologist listening in comes alive with interest. In sev-
enteen years of lion study in the field, he has never observed a cat
that did not sense his presence. And now he is talking to a man who
has caught lions in the act of love.

"Yep," grins the rancher, "And I want you to know that I'm
enough of a cowman that I shot the female first."

Fish

THE OLD MAN DRAGS ON HIS CAMEL and says, "Yes, John Slaughter sat in front of that window every evening."

The old man does not like me and I do not like him. But I am here from a newspaper and have gotten the permission of his boss, so he can do little. He barks at his wife, he sneers at me. My hair is long, my jacket, boots, and manner give the image of that despicable entity, the backpacker, bird-watcher, nature lover. For me, he is that persistent fraud, the creature who cherishes a bedtime story called "The Winning of the West." He feeds off anger, hate, and dreams of conquest. Just a little while ago, he caught me down by the pond staring at a vermilion flycatcher through my binoculars. He will never forgive that moment.

The enormous living room feels like a fort. Slaughter rebuilt with thick walls after the earthquake of May 3, 1887, toppled the old house. The adobe building held the headquarters of the San Bernardino Ranch, a spread seventeen miles east of Douglas, Arizona, on the Mexican line. Slaughter's land ran to 65,000 acres of an old Spanish land grant.

The old house on the old grant is a memory of an old dream called the Old West. And the old man smoking his Camel is a full-time dreamer. He is stuffed with lore about John Slaughter, Texas John Slaughter, the Sheriff of Cochise, the man who died of old age in 1922 and reappeared as a television series in the fifties. Listening to him is like punching a tape recorder and then being hammered by an insistent, hectoring voice.

John—the old man always calls him John—sat right over there by the window and read every night. He wore a big Stetson hat. Only that night—and here he pauses for another drag—that night he'd lost his hat in a bet with his foreman, Jesse Fisher.

Here the story gets complicated. The old man must detail the bet, the losing of the bet, the look of the yard in the twilight. Everything must be said in its proper order like a ritual prayer.

And then Jesse, wearing Slaughter's hat, walked across the back to the commissary. The light was failing and they shot him dead. The killers thought they'd gotten John Slaughter, but of course they had not. Nobody would ever get John.

The ranch has changed a lot since Slaughter's day. The family eventually sold out and now it has been whittled down to 2400 acres. Once Slaughter owned 50,000 head. Tonight there is not one cow on the place. They are not permitted.

The San Bernardino has been bought so that it can be saved and cherished. But not because of John Slaughter. This is what rankles the old man. He cannot fathom it. He is a caretaker for the temporary owners, the Nature Conservancy, who will soon unload the ranch house on a historical foundation and the land on a federal agency. The Nature Conservancy does not care much about the ranch's place in the Old West. They bought the spread and kicked the cows off to preserve a creature John Slaughter never put his brand on: the Yaqui topminnow, *Poeciliopsis occidentalis sonoriensis*.

The fish is an inch or two long and very shy. When I was down by the pond earlier it scurried away in the weeds. The leaves trembled as the minnows darted past as shadows beneath the glass surface.

They have no known value to man and they are almost extinct. Nobody ever whipped out a frying pan upon sighting a Yaqui topminnow. Sportsmen do not mount them in their dens. Very few human beings on the surface of the earth realize they exist.

John Slaughter is dead and the land around his ranch house is all but dead. The Yaqui topminnow lives, here and in a few other places.

The old man snuffs out his cigarette. He cannot understand the goddamn interest in the fish. Now John Slaughter, he was something. He was a man. Slaughter, he says, could sense danger. After all he knew when not to wear his Stetson. And he was tough. They say the night of the Jesse Fisher killing he sat up with a gun waiting out his enemies in the darkness. That's the history of it, the old man finishes. He is devoted to John, a kind of private religion.

Bird song floats up from the pond. Ruddy ducks storm across the top of the water, flycatchers cartwheel off limbs pursuing bugs, and among the lily pads frogs stare with headlight eyes as night washes over the range. Here and there a topminnow flashes.

The old man wonders what in the hell it is all about.

The body of a Yaqui topminnow runs from tan to olive, darkest on top, yellow to white below. The males are larger than the females and when it comes to breeding, a brood may run from six to fortynine and gestation takes only about two weeks.

The Yaqui topminnow, along with many fish native to Arizona, is endangered because it has run out of places to live. In the southern part of the state, the rivers are mainly dead and the cienegas— swamps—have vanished. In Mexico, the fish once flourished throughout the Yaqui river basin, a drainage that reaches from Slaughter's ranch down to the Gulf of California near Obregon, Sonora.

Farms, people, and cattle have dried the river up and the minnow has become rare. North of the border, the fish has retreated to a couple of artesian wells on the San Bernardino ranch. Even here life has been exciting. A big minnow population at the ranch's Astin Spring was wiped out in 1969 when cattle trampled the area to dust during a dry year.

The Nature Conservancy collects plants, birds, bugs, fish, reptiles, mammals—all kinds of life that are unique and threatened by the rush of American life. They bought the ranch because that seemed the only way of saving the fish. And John Slaughter's ghost came along as part of the baggage.

Species today are disappearing at the rate of about one hundred a year or more. As growing numbers of human beings move in and gobble the remaining rain forests, deserts, bogs, forests, prairies, plains and the sea, the kill rate is expected to be 100 a day for the next twenty years, or about 40,000 species a year. Scientists figure there are 5 to 10 million species on earth so the extermination can go on for a long time.

This is the current the Yaqui topminnow must swim against. For over a century, the fish has been in training at the San Bernardino for such adversity.

Indians had been drawn to the springs for thousands of years and then Spaniards drifted through in the sixteenth and seventeenth centuries noting pastures, scouting gold, and bagging a few converts. The great captain of the Southwest, De Anza, camped here in 1773 while on an Apache hunt. Jesuits founded a mission that took up three acres and left a legend of buried gold to fire the blood of later dreamers.

In 1820, Lieut. Ignacio de Perez bought the San Bernardino grant for $90. This was a bit steep for the time since the outfit had been appraised at $60. But he bit the bullet and plunked down the money for 75,000 acres. Grass carpeted the ground and soon Perez had installed 100,000 cattle, 10,000 horses, and 5000 mules. For ten years, he prospered. Then Arizona's persistent conservationists, the Apaches, put the prod to the Spaniards. The settlers fled south and the cattle went wild.

The San Bernardino drifted out of written history for awhile. American soldiers marched through in 1846 on their way to California. They were looking for a piece of the Mexican War.

"The ox, in a perfectly wild state, abound here," a commander noted.

Three years later, H. M. T. Powell and a group of gold rush hopefuls from Illinois found the springs a haven full of mean bulls. Cattle tracks led off everywhere and a big bear prowled around the Spanish ruins.

John R. Bartlett of the Boundary Commission paused here in 1854. He, too, was taken aback by the herds. But having only a pair of pistols and a double-barreled shotgun, he left the cattle alone. The springs fed green swales of grass and herons exploded from the ponds.

All the accounts echo the same delight at finding water after long dry marches and the same horror at discovering cows and bulls that had escaped human control and use.

This was the ground John Slaughter bought in 1884. Soon he had

50,000 head wearing his brand. He drilled wells and made more ponds. From 1887 to 1890, he served as Sheriff of Cochise County, a renowned hellhole of thieves, cutthroats, gamblers, rustlers, and towns like Tombstone. Slaughter created a new standard for law enforcement. When he set out after a badman, he generally did not return with a prisoner and the fellow he went after was usually never seen again. Apparently, three years of this approach wiped out the need for his skills.

By the 1890s, he was a successful cowman with vast herds, the big ranch, the wonderful wells. He was living the dream of his time. Grass poured through the guts of his steers and turned into dollars.

This was part of winning the place called the West.

Now walls of dust sweep across the valley. Down below, the ranch house lies hidden in a draw. Up on the mesa, where I stand, a monument begs for attention by the dirt road. The inscription reads "Mormon Battalion, San Bernardino Ranch Rest Camp, Dec. 6, 1846." Shards of broken beer bottles litter the ground around the obelisk and nearby a white thorn acacia cowers from the wind.

The San Bernardino ranch is pocked with the efforts of men to claim it. The rise where the Mormon Battalion bunked for the night was once called *Mesa de la Avanzada,* mesa of the advanced guard, when Spaniards from the Presidio of Fronteras bunked here too. Just above the ranch house are the remains of barracks Black Jack Pershing used when his men hunted Pancho Villa in the fun days before Americans faced the trenches and machine guns of World War I. Everybody who passed through here slapped names on the ground, got greedy glints in their eyes at the possibilities of the springs and grasslands and then drifted off to nowhere or into history books.

Down below in the springs and ponds, the fish struggled. First, the use by people and cattle reduced the amount of water and butchered their numbers. Then mosquito fish were introduced in the twentieth century to control mosquitoes. They wiped out many of the native fish when they proved better at taking the available food.

Besides the Yaqui topminnow, the ranch became a holding action for the Yaqui chub, Yaqui catfish, Beautiful Shiner, and Mexican Stoneroller. When the Nature Conservancy bought the place in 1979, the chub was down to about twenty survivors. They lived in a pipe near a spring and when a man approached they would flee back into the pipe. Now they number 30,000.

For the fish, a new truce is in the offing. The Nature Conservancy eventually turned the land over to the U.S. Fish and Wildlife Service and that agency has plans to restore the ranch. The dream is for the return of tall grass, thickets of cane, and mucky bogs. The hayfields have been abandoned, the cows sent home.

The San Bernardino is heading for a time before John Slaughter, before the gold seekers and the Mormon Battalion, before Perez or the Jesuits. The ranch is drifting toward some imaginary day before Christopher Columbus docked in what came to be called the New World.

Before that vision of a golden past can be reached, there are some fierce times that must be erased from the land. Drought came in 1892 and 1893 and the great herds died of thirst and hunger. Slaughter had temporarily to mortgage the ranch. Bone gatherers came to the San Bernardino. They piled skulls and leg bones into pyramids and then pitched the heaps onto trains for the fertilizer factories back East.

Slaughter rebounded from this disaster but the land lacked his bounce. In the 1850s, a creek meandered east of the ranch house with cottonwoods along its banks. Grassland stretched away from it. Then the creek became a kind of ditch used by Slaughter to water his fields. Today this ditch is called Black Draw. The banks are sheer drops of ten to twenty feet. The Draw is almost always dry. The former fields and marshlands are now mesquite thickets and bare trampled earth.

A hundred years ago Black Draw had no name because Black Draw did not exist. In the West, there is a tendency to accept the big landscape as a timeless benchmark of continuity. This does not give our ancestors proper credit for their drive and energy.

Slaughter's people sold out in the thirties and after a couple of more owners, grass had given way to mesquite and bare earth. There was not much else but cattle, those exotic monsters Americans love to put out on the land so that everywhere they look, they can delight in seeing the same biological monotony.

The ranch house itself is a kind of curio of the glory days and a sign out by the dirt road proudly announces this to be the Slaughter Ranch. Overhead, hawks wheel and hunt rodents on the ruined range. At the springs and artesian wells, the Yaqui topminnow feeds and awaits the next news bulletin.

Over by Black Draw, the new feel of the place slaps the eye. Tumbleweeds pile up against the fences and fill the deep gouge like some local variety of cotton candy. Tumbleweeds thrive on disturbed soil and the San Bernardino is lush with tumbleweeds.

The plant personifies much of the American West. They are everywhere, they are recent and they say this ground has been looted. They are the corpses of Russian thistle, a plant that is said to have entered the United States in a bag of imported wheat seed in the 1870s. It first showed up in the Dakotas and by the 1890s had reached the East Coast. The thistle went everywhere that people disturbed the land which meant it went just about everywhere.

Two potent symbols of the frontier—cattle and tumbleweeds—are as American as, well, borscht.

The American West was a kind of sweet dream for the Russian thistle. Now it has entered song and no one who claims to love the West can separate the region from the tumbling tumbleweeds. They are the cherished mark Americans have made on their native ground. So many other marks can be overlooked or missed. Few have ears keen enough to catch the bellows of the millions of dead buffalo, the wingbeats of hundreds of millions of dead passenger pigeons or the faint swish as a Yaqui topminnow darts by.

The tumbleweed, almost by default, has to do a lot of the talking in the New West about the Old West. The brittle bundles roll across America linking the quaint West of the Gunbelt with the booming West of the Sunbelt.

I push through the mesquite and a flat, empty space opens beside Black Draw. The ground is bare dirt with here and there tiny sprouts of new thistles. This is an abandoned field now getting some rest. In a few years the thistles will leave. They cannot thrive unless the ground is constantly disturbed by plows or hooves. Along the edge of the field, a sparrow hawk sits in a dead cottonwood waiting for something to make a move.

The wind blows with a steady moan. To the east, the map suggests North Pond should be found but nothing can be seen but a wall of tumbleweeds piled up against some mesquites.

The hawk lifts off.

I am witnessing an ancient and endless newsreel. Since life began on earth 3.5 million years ago, about 100 to 250 million species have tried the place out. Between ninety and ninety-eight percent of these efforts failed and became extinct.

The Yaqui topminnow is but one of many stabs at life and it may soon join this parade of failed designs. What alarms some people is not extinction but the rate of extinction. A million species may disappear in the next twenty-five years, largely because of human activity. No one is quite sure what will happen if the variety of living things declines that rapidly.

But one thing is certain: the earth is getting more monotonous. The total weight of all human beings is about 200 million tons. Insects still weight ten to twelve times this amount but people are gaining. Right now, for what it's worth, people equal the weight of all the krill in the oceans. Or try looking at it another way. About 30,000 years ago, there were maybe 10 million people on earth and millions of orangutans. Consider a France with 6000 people, the population at about the time the famous cave paintings began being created.

People are forging a natural world that mirrors the exciting possibilities of the subdivisions thrown up after World War II. Variety—what scientists like to call diversity—is disappearing. Increasingly a few species hog the space of a complex web of species. The grasses of the Great Plains give way to wheat, the strains of wheat give way to a couple of renditions of superwheat. Back on the San Bernardino, a wonderland of marshes and grassland surrenders to the simplicity of Russian thistle and mesquite.

For people who hate to learn the names of things, the world is getting better every day.

Against this wave of the future, ecologists, nature lovers, and assorted cranks mount a few arguments. They say a world with fewer species is less beautiful. They say a world with fewer species is less stable. And they say a world with fewer species is immoral. Nobody pays much attention to these arguments.

Finally, as a hole card, the defenders of endangered species say that someday, somewhere, the threatened organisms may have an economic value. They point out that the genetic pool is a warehouse worth keeping chock-full. Sometimes they hint that some fish or bug or weed or beast may hold the cure for cancer.

Anyone can pick and choose among these arguments. Whatever feels best is fine, because the pressure of human numbers and human appetites promises to eliminate species wholesale and all the arguments are probably beside the point.

The best argument is undoubtedly the one that impresses the fewest people and convinces hardly anyone at all: Species are worth saving because a world with less life is less of a world.

The mosquito, Yaqui topminnow, great white shark, bedbug, and prickly pear cactus are all worth having around.

Life is not about industrial economies at the tail end of the second millennium. Life is a long-term crap game and the house rules should give everyone a roll with the dice. Imagine that the destiny of the planet is not increasing the Gross National Product or making life nicer for human beings or easier for Yaqui topminnows. Imagine that it is a mystery. Think how puzzled the tens of millions of vanished species must feel about the purpose of life.

The endangered and often useless species are messengers and what they report to us is that the world is not especially designed for people or progress or machines or civilization. That is why these organisms and plants are resented. The snail darters of the earth are not despised simply because they might stall the construction of a dam. They are hated because they suggest by their very existence that the planet is not solely a habitat put together to benefit human beings.

Every time a great white shark glides past, people have to wonder just what in the hell life is really about. A world empty of useless species will be a world with fewer tough questions.

And so the planet is becoming a better place for people who hurt their heads when they think.

At Black Draw, the hard questions have not yet been silenced. The sun stands at noon, the wind continues blasting across the bare ground, and everywhere cracks lance the dry earth. At the edge of the field along Black Draw, the sparrow hawk has returned to the tree without a kill. A small seep fingers out from a pile of tumbleweed and muddies up a patch of earth. It is difficult to remember that once the grass stood high, the cattle grew fat, a lonely bear prowled the old Spanish ruins, and herons fished the marshes here.

Just before the edge of the seep is reached a sound erupts and a flock of mallards explodes into the sky. They storm upward from the hidden surface of North Pond.

And then a great blue heron lifts off and undulates just above the mesquite like a slate gray wraith drifting across the parched bones of the San Bernardino ranch.

We are walking down the road in Sonora just below the American line. To the south stretches the Pinacate, a black volcanic wilderness, to the north the Cabeza Prieta refuge. My body lumbers along and there are aches from last night's sleep on a field of stones. All my water is gone and the 110-degree August sun bakes me to an even turn.

I have come fifty miles and I think of cold beer. Last night a boy on horseback, a kid we knew from earlier forays, came upon us. He is bewitched by us and has named his saddle horse, mochila, backpack. He sat there in the twilight, frowned, and said, "Do not continue. The snakes will be out. The snakes once got my favorite horse." He asked us to go to his home. We could see the brick hut off in the distance, the family cooking over a mesquite fire. But the desert tugged and the feet kept moving. The last good water was a tank with bloated dead toads floating on the surface. We drank deeply.

I walk for hours and notice nothing but my thirst and fatigue and hunger. Nothing stirs, not a breeze, bird, insect, or lizard. This is the killing time.

Cars and trucks fly by but I hardly notice.

I come across a road-killed coyote. The ribs and vertebrae and femurs are all in place but the meat and skin have vanished. Except for the head. Magically, the hide is intact on the head and empty eyes stare out at another desert day.

The lips are curled back from the teeth.

The coyote is smiling.

PLAYERS

Of course, there were killings.

—Glendolene Myrtle Kimmell,
a friend of Tom Horn, April 12, 1904

The woman spins in a column of red light while six speakers rub her body with sound. The breasts are small, the hips heavy and she is circled by a dozen men devouring her gestures in the roadside bar. It is nearly 5 P.M. on Monday night, just four days since a drug deal went bad in the bar's business office.

The jukebox says

> Money talks
> It don't sing and dance
> And it don't walk

She climbs off the stage in plastic heels and sucks on a glowing cigarette. Dollar bills peak from her G-string and she wears a black arm band in remembrance. The next dancer steps up and pulls off her shirt. The men stare.

Last Thursday night two men in the back room closed out a deal. Clifford Hamilton, thirty-three, was a one-legged member of the Huns, a motorcycle gang. The other man was a narc.

Four ounces of cocaine drew them together. In the bar, a dancer swayed before an audience salted with police. A signal was given, the cops moved.

Tonight there are no cops, just the music and the flesh. The naked woman washes over the blank features of the men like a summer rain. A ballad comes up with easy guitar chords,

> Some say love is a razor
> That leaves your soul to bleed

The woman's face stretches taut across her features like a mask. She bends and the breasts hang. A man rises wobbly from a table and walks to the stage. The woman squats, lifts her G-string and he drops a buck into the warmth of her crotch.

The barmaid circulates gathering money for the dancers and a new song struggles through the blue air.

> Gonna harden my heart
> Gonna swallow my tears.

A bank of horns soars behind the lyrics. Dark-paneled walls reach up to a brown ceiling. The naked woman never smiles. The men never stir. Her breasts are perfect.

Four days ago, the first cop through the door held a shotgun. He looked and dove to the floor. The second cop was plainclothes narcotics. Clifford Hamilton turned from his desk with a .9mm semi-automatic pistol. He pulled the trigger and lead flew down the barrel at roughly 1,200 miles an hour. The second cop, Jeffrey Ross, 27, took the slug in his chest and died.

The woman dancing tonight glows with sweat, her skin a white snack set off by that black armband. The new song says

Born to be wiiild.

The dancer says, "This one's for Clifford."

The men do not respond. The naked woman laughs, "Be happy you weren't in the bar four nights ago."

That time the cops poured through the door of the business office and a 12-gauge shotgun roared thirty-four pellets down its barrel at around 1,100 miles an hour. The cluster swished through the air in a six-inch circle and ripped through Hamilton's body ten feet away. The bullets kept coming and no one kept count. When the cops came through the door, they said Hamilton was counting the cash. Four ounces of coke were supposedly worth $10,000 on the street.

Tonight, the dancer smiles at the men who lick her body with their eyes. She puts a quarter in the jukebox and says, "This was one of Clifford's favorites."

I'm just a soul whose intentions are good.
Oh, Lord, please don't let me be misunderstood.

At the bar, it is the heart of the Happy Hour.

Escalante

FRANK ESCALANTE FEELS the ground vanishing beneath his feet and before his world disappears he wants just one thing: to find his brother's grave. He looks up the hill from his small ranch on the east side of Tucson and sees tract houses streaming down the slope toward Pantano Wash. Nearby, the government lopped off forty acres of his land for a dump. Across the hills to the south, his people once worked at Rancho del Lago, an ancient spread now being bulldozed into a lake-studded resort with a golf course.

He warns, "Don't go there, they have cut down the cottonwoods, they have destroyed everything."

Escalante is nearing sixty with black hair, a trim, thin mustache and the lean body of a horseman. Three grown sons live on his land with their own homes, families, and children. To the east, his two sisters have their place. Up the slope to the southeast, another sister lives behind an ocotillo fence. Her son and daughter are also clustered around her in their own houses. It is a way of life.

But it is not my life. Tucson officially prides itself on deep Hispanic roots. The Chamber of Commerce likes to label the metropolis "The Old Pueblo" and the annual rodeo ventures forth as the *Fiesta de los Vaqueros*. Officially, Mexicans are an asset like blue skies, big mountains, loose real estate laws, and feeble trade unions. Of course this whole stance is an amiable fraud.

When I was a high school student in the early sixties, speaking Spanish was forbidden on the campus lest the natives relay secret messages. For a century, the Anglo world has crushed and buried the Mexican. Sometimes by hook or crook but mainly by an overwhelming application of money, energy, and human numbers. The Anglos forge nuclear families or no families at all. The Mexicans persist in trying to maintain extended families and chase goals that do not easily coincide with profits, condominiums, and constant movement from city to city, state to state. In the best sense of the word, they have remained un-American.

I am tied to this booming, ugly city but every time I meet someone like Escalante I realize how shallow my commitment is. My bags are always packed.

The Escalantes are mixed into this ground like straw and mud in adobe block. A nearby road bears their name. They have lived on Tucson's eastside for 100 years. It was not the eastside then but simply the land.

And in that ground, Frank Escalante knows his brother's body rests. He wants to find it. He has paid men to search for it, to dig holes that promised bones. He has looked hard himself. It is somewhere over there he points, there near that brick house with the tile roof, there where a new row of houses marches down the wash.

Escalante knows his brother is on that real estate development because his mother told him.

It happened this way. She was plowing the field with a mule and a horse hitched together. She was breaking the horse to the work. Then the pains came and no one else was around. The kids were at school, her husband off hauling sand and gravel. She left the field and delivered the child herself. It was a boy and he was born dead.

Escalante's mother got a flour sack and put the body in it. Then she dug a grave and buried the baby.

Frank Escalante wants to find that grave, he wants to put his brother in the family burying ground out on Old Spanish Trail. He is a man determined to keep his past and his family together.

Now he must hurry. Much of his land is leased and the state keeps fiddling and fussing about his use of it. The day is almost over when a Mexican can live in a simple house along a wash and run a little stock, have a small garden, appreciate the lines of a good horse. The city has come and soon Escalante's world will disappear into a new thing called the eastside.

He lives in what has the look of a modern ranch-style house. The kitchen is vast, the living room centered on an enormous television. The fireplace takes up one wall.

"Me and the kids," he says through a smile, "built this place with stuff from the dump."

The block is salvaged, the huge porch beams once held up a bridge—he is finishing the ceiling with saguaro ribs found in the desert. Out in the yard among roses and chrysanthemums is a weeping mulberry. He found it uprooted at the dump. The lawn grew from a clump he plucked at a new shopping center.

Around the main house are his sons' houses and the rodeo grounds with bleachers for the fans and a tower for the judges. Huge stables are going up. Everything comes from the dump. Frank Escalante wastes nothing, not his past, not his present.

For a doorstop he uses his mother's old corn-grinding mano. Out in the yard, he has her mill. His son is restoring her old iron bed.

Escalante was born in a different kind of house. A man would set four mesquite posts into the ground and then place some beams across. He'd roof with saguaro ribs and cardboard and dirt. The walls would be woven with sticks and then plastered with mud. When Frank was a baby, his cradle hung by a chain from just such a mesquite post. He still has the chain and he can walk across his land and take a visitor to the post.

Both sides of his family came up from Ures, Sonora. He does not know exactly when but his grandmother used to tell him tales of the gold rush of 1849. His grandfather, Manuel, married Dolores Lauterio and the couple had twenty-five children. One son, also named Manuel, was born in 1885. He married Florentina whose father owned 160 acres along Pantano Wash and he grazed his cattle all over what is now the huge Davis Monthan Air Force Base. Manuel's brother Miguel owned a slaughterhouse and was a partner in ventures with rich Tucson Anglos like the Steinfelds. He became a big landowner.

The throng of Escalantes penetrated the canyons and grazing lands of the Rincon Mountains that tower over Tucson to the east. They are buried all over the range in abandoned graveyards.

A small folk industry centered on working lime kilns. The men would dig a hole, fill it up with rocks and wood and then let the wood burn for a day or two. That is how they made lime. The hills today are pocked with the holes of the kilns.

"What my grandfather used to do for a living," Frank says, "was to have these lime kilns—in fact that is the way he died."

The old man was bringing in a wagonload with Frank's uncle who was then a boy. The Pantano was running and the wagon got stuck. The old man started carrying off bags of lime to lighten the load and had a heart attack. He sat under a tree by the wash and died. The boy went off and found a cowboy and they brought his body home. That was 1909.

His father, Manuel, homesteaded the current Escalante land in 1916.

He lights a smoke and stabs to the northeast with the cigarette. "I was born right over there. It was just a mud hut where I was born."

His mother was once again working in the fields; she could work like a man, he recalls. She felt the pains and took the team to the edge of the plowed ground and tied them to a palo verde tree. Then she walked to the house.

She said Frank just dropped, as easy as that, and then she cut the cord and tied it off. She set the baby on a blanket. His mother then thought of the horses tied up out there in the heat. She went and got them and brought them in. Then she cleansed her baby.

The land meant work. The family raised its own food—corn, lentils, beans, chiles, tobacco. His mother made cheese, saguaro fruit provided jam, and honey came from their hives. The children all had jobs to do. Frank would get up at 4 A.M. and drive a wagonload of wood ten miles into town. His father salvaged the cordwood from drift left by the floods of the Pantano. The boy would guide his team to where the modern Community Center now stands. In the 1930s a community occupied the same ground. His major competition was Papagos peddling mesquite. Frank got $1.75 a load if things went well. He would get back home around 8 at night and his father would load the wagon while he slept. At 4 A.M. he headed back into town.

Frank Escalante at the time was ten years old.

The family had five children and no car. They made everything they needed or did without. Water was hauled in barrels from a well four miles away. When it rained, they captured every drop they could from the Pantano. They would squeeze out the tadpoles with a cloth and wait for the mud to settle.

Expenses nibbled away at the land. Once his father sold 160 acres for $60. But in the main, the family existed detached from the growing state of Arizona. They lived in a different entity, the Sonoran Desert. They were part of a great living thing that has since been buried alive by the economic spree called Sunbelt.

"When I started school," Escalante recalls, "I didn't even know how to say in English how to go to the restroom."

He attended a one-room schoolhouse and carried his lunch in an old lard can. What he knew in those days was how to rodeo, how to ranch, how to farm, how to haul wood, make lime, and harvest wild plants.

Then in his eighteenth year, the world knocked and he went to a brand new school.

World War II.

The Army taught him welding, automotive repair, painting, and killing. In Texas, he discovered he was a Mexican when a cafe refused to serve him a cup of coffee. Escalante also learned "that a man could make himself into almost anything he wants to."

He was a forward artillery spotter, and he walked across France into Germany. Brief memories surface. He was sent to bring in the bodies of two buddies. He wrapped his face with rags but a tiny gap in the cloth exposed his neck. The stench hung on his skin for what seemed like weeks. Toward the end of the war, his outfit came up against an entrenched German position. Escalante glassed the menacing troops and called down a barrage. When they took the position, they found the bodies of German children thirteen or fourteen years old, kids conscripted into the final defense of the Reich.

He was with the first troops to stumble on the death camps, the bodies stacked like cords of mesquite back home. In the states, he trained with a unit of 150 men. When the war ended in Europe, nine were alive. He was immediately put in a combat unit for the expected assault on the home islands of Japan. The surrender found him still in Austria where he became an interpreter and married an Austrian girl.

In 1947, he returned to his father's land and he and his wife began building their house with material scavenged from the dump. They raised five sons and Frank got a job at the nearby Air Force base that had boomed with the war. He learned to be an aircraft mechanic.

After the war, he never ranched for a living. The family sold off another 160 acres in the late forties for $4000. The slide toward an unimagined future continued. One day, in 1953, Frank Escalante jumped down off the wing of a plane and injured his knee. Surgery followed and he had to retire on a disability pension. He got a job working on the county roads and stayed fourteen years. The knee became a curse and he peddled parcel after parcel to pay for operations that never restored the joint.

His father died in 1967 at age eighty-four. He'd been feeding his cattle the morning of his death. Each child got 20 acres. Today, after his medical bills, Frank Escalante is down to 5 acres plus 104 more leased from the state. The small town to the west where he sold cord wood as a child is now a city of over half a million and surrounds him.

He half ignores this fact and continues chasing the image of his own world where people live on the land and slowly improvise small statements of their lives. A new patio wall is going up and Escalante, now often on crutches, scoots along the ground putting in a footing. He wants his house in order.

The old family burying ground has fallen into disrepair. Escalante inherited the tract several miles east of his ranch along the Rincon Mountains.

"I'm not going to let it go," he says adamantly, "because all my great grandparents and everybody is buried there."

He has staged rodeos at his ranch to raise money for restoring the old graveyard. Crowds of a thousand attended and dined on beef pit barbecued from two slaughtered steers. Escalante is strict about such matters. The cattle would be killed next to the pit, the hole filled with mesquite. When the wood burned down, he lowered meat wrapped in hides. No metal must ever touch the meat. Ever.

With the money raised from the rodeos, Escalante repaired the cemetery wall and built a ramada where mass can be said on All Soul's Day. There is an impressive gate and tiled image of the Virgin of Guadelupe.

The small graveyard sits on a desert knoll and twelve bouquets of plastic flowers hang off the gate. A hitching post stands by the flag pole. Many of the wooden crosses tilt and more have crumbled back into dust. A poured slab covers the grave of Dolores Lauterio de Escalante, 1863 – 1934, the woman who bore twenty-five children, the mother of them all.

Mountains tower across the valley and cars roar by on a paved highway. Just down the road, the adobe home of Frank's uncle slowly bleeds back into the earth. The Rincons are thick with memory—Frank's grandfather helped surveyors map the range and hauled a stove up to the top for the first fire watchers. Everywhere Escalante looks he sees traces of his blood. And everywhere he looks he sees trouble.

The rodeos had to be discontinued because the crowds drank liquor and smoked pot and stole things from the ranch. The graveyard has been vandalized and the headstones stand amid a litter of broken beer bottles.

But these are all minor matters compared to other threats. The Escalante land is now surrounded by city or the dreams of the city. IBM has placed a big factory just to the south and developers smell money in the creosote. Escalante runs eight head of cattle on his parcel. The state is mandated to get a maximum return from its holdings and eight head does not stack up against a subdivision or a factory.

So the matter is cut and dried. But for Escalante it is not so simple. Land being taken from Mexicans awakens old wounds, and he will not meekly accept the end of adobe houses, old graveyards, and a few head of cattle scouting out a living on the desert flats. He was raised on stories of local Mexicans framed by Anglos so that their land could be seized. He remembers a neighbor of his grandfather who had rustled hides planted in his corral, hides put there, the story goes, by the legendary Arizona Rangers.

The lawmen surrounded his place at night and the man snuck off to the Escalante ranch. His grandfather went out to the corral and saddled a horse by lantern light. The man vanished into Mexico, his land forfeited. The same trick was later tried on Frank's grandfather but the old man knew a good lawyer and beat the charge.

These are the lessons handed down in old time Mexican families like the Escalantes. The Anglos came and the land was eaten away. It is no longer a point for historians to quibble over and prove or disprove. It is long past that. It is now a belief mingled with the blood.

"The rich have always stomped the poor," Escalante calmly notes. "From that mountain to this mountain, all across this valley where Tucson sprawls, the land used to be Mexican owned."

Some was lost to back taxes, much was taken by the Forest Service, and some fell victim to hides planted in the night. And now for Escalante, more is likely to be lost because the terms of a lease held fifty years are suddenly changing.

He is the last of a long roll call. Escalante has the old brand book for the area. Vanished Mexican ranchers and the symbols burned into their cattle are recorded in longhand: the Riesgos, a thundering herd of Escalantes, the families Benitez, Molina, Conteras, Queroz, Carrillo, Figueroa, Mendez, Martinez, Tellez, and others.

He thinks he will move, find some backwater county and relocate. He will pack up all his treasures and his family and sell out. But moving may not be so simple. There is the matter of his brother's lost grave. There are all those graves out along Old Spanish Trail. There is that buck rake out in the yard that his father bought from Ronstadt's Hardware in 1925—he cannot part with that. Or the coffee grinder over the fireplace that a *Villista* had on his boxcar during the Revolution. And out in the yard is another corn grinder Frank got from a Yaqui witch.

He rummages through old photographs and offers images of the mud hut where he was born ("that's where my cradle hung"), a long-dead horse ("I could make him walk a 100 feet on his hind legs"). He grabs his crutches and goes outside. His eight-year-old grandson tags along. On the porch of one son's house, he has hung all his father's old tools—traps for coyotes and foxes, stirrups, a gun, skulls, a pack saddle, a bridle.

A metal fence snakes along with old tools welded to the top, and the gallery centers on a crucifix. A steel pot hangs below waiting for flowers. Bits of old wagons lie about like bones of vanished beasts. The boy pokes a single tree and asks, "What's this?"

Down the lane a bit, an old adobe wall falls back to earth—his father's barn.

"I won't touch it," Escalante says, "I just let it fall."

The front fence is lined with more old farming tools. Escalante stops and points up at a jagged rock on the Rincons and says there are rock drawings there and an old Indian campground. A path, he continues, leads from the drawings, almost as if the images were supposed to show the way. The path ends in a sheer cliff.

He lights a smoke and stares up the hills of advancing houses. His grandson is at his side as he explains where his father farmed, where he farmed, and where his grandfather and great grandfather farmed.

The smoke curls from his lips as he announces, "I can't live here anymore."

But first he must find his brother's grave.

His black eyes gleam and the coarse hair hangs down his back like rope. He speaks softly, almost a mumble, and he tells me that his people, the Papago people, the Tohono O'odham *have traditions, sacred ways, and that the earth is sacred to them and the water is sacred to them and life is sacred to them also.*

His strong arms hang from his sleeveless t-shirt and his chest heaves under his black vest. He lives in the western part of the reservation, a Connecticut-sized chunk of southern Arizona that on any given day hosts perhaps 15,000 Indians. He is married to a white woman and she parrots his words with a whiskey voice.

I listen carefully.

His hands have prison tattoos. He has just finished ten or twelve years in the big house. When he was a teenager, he lived with his aunt and uncle. One day, he crawled up on a hillside by his village and sighted down his deer rifle and his aunt and uncle dropped like stones. For that he got ten or twelve years.

Now he has found himself, he says. He no longer lives in that village but in a more ancient one up in the mountains. The community had been abandoned and he is bringing it back to life with his presence.

He wants to tell me of the traditional ways and why the current offers being made to the tribe for water rights and land rights must be spurned.

They violate the sacred ways, the traditions, he drones on.

I think of these words as I stare at his jailhouse tattoos.

Rios

RIOS HAS STORIES about rich Indians and deals made with whites.

"I haven't had a hard life," he says, "I've suffered, it hasn't been glorious. But I know people who have really suffered."

In the sixties, he continues, ASARCO, a big copper company, made the San Xavier Papagos an offer on land for a waste dump. Some tribal members received small sums, some much more.

In one family, the husband got $18,000 and then shortly afterward he shot himself. His widow started running around with another guy who also had received $18,000. That man hanged himself. Then the widow split for Los Angeles, bought a new pickup and drove back to San Xavier. A truck wreck crushed her head like an egg.

Her son insisted on opening the coffin. The sight broke him. The troubles kept coming. The son caught his wife in bed with another man, stabbed her and left her paralyzed for life. Then his son hung himself.

Rios pauses in his account. He speaks in a monotone and the words slip out in a bland swirl of sounds.

"That," he says, "is a hard life."

But at the moment, it is the good life that has him worried. His stubby fingers guide a red pencil under dark lines of type. Black hair tumbles down his rich brown forehead and Mike Rios continues to pore over a fifty-three-page proposed lease for some Papago land touching Tucson's Sunbelt sprawl. His hotel room in Palm Springs has soft colors, thick rugs, heavy drapes. Peter Thomas, twenty-two,

69

his friend, sits on the bed watching television. The sound is off and a huge tape recorder floods the room with Papago chicken scratch music, a Sonoran Desert kind of polka.

Rios ignores the television, ignores the Indian band fuming with mesquite smoke, ignores everything but the lease. Outside the sliding glass doors, Palm Springs shrugs off the day. Joggers totter past in perfectly matched running outfits and homes for the rich creep up the hillsides and wrap themselves in cocoons of oleanders and palms. Mercedes clog the street. It is not easy being both rich and original.

Rios is hunting, stalking his quarry through the wilderness of the fine print lease, looking for that clause that spells ruin for his tribe. He can't prove it is there but he senses its presence on some deep level. He can see the ruin out the window of the Sun Royal Hotel. Palm Springs is stuffed with 36,000 white people. Once it was exclusively Indian ground.

Now this possibility of a boom hangs over his home in the San Xavier district of the Papago reservation. James J. Rothschild, Jr., president of Santa Cruz Properties, Inc., has made an offer to the 1,000 Papagos who live in the district. He wants a sixty-five-year lease with the possibility of a thirty-five-year extension on 18,000 acres of Papago ground so that he can build a community for 110,000 white people. The tract is convenient to the freeway and airport and a quick spin from downtown Tucson.

For months, he has lobbied the tribal council, held meetings with the people at San Xavier, flown tribal representatives to Palm Springs. He says he is ready to make his plan cement. All he needs is permission.

On paper the offer promises to make the Papagos rich. The offers always do. Rios wonders. He can give many reasons for his doubts but they all rest on one big reason: he does not trust white people. Rothschild has dealt with other Indians in the past, namely the Agua Caliente band of Palm Springs. He is but one of many developers who has transformed land in this area into a playground for the rich. It seems a natural progression—Rothschild himself merely represents rich Canadians looking for a place to park their millions. So he cuts deals and spins dreams.

Rios has driven to Palm Springs to discover what all the promises look like when they have become condos, golf courses, and country clubs. He wants to talk to the Agua Calientes about Rothschild, to learn the intricacies of leases, to study the risks of development and to be coached on how Indians can sign contracts with whites.

But before he tackles these matters, he sits in his hotel room at a table underlining sentences in the big lease while chicken scratch music washes over him and the television flickers at his back. The drive from Tucson took eight hours, a lot of Coors and tape after tape of chicken scratch. But Rios, 44, has come much further than that.

His father abandoned him at age two and he did not know who his mother was until age twelve. He lived with his grandparents on a ranch and ate a lot of beans and tortillas. Meat was a hit-and-miss affair.

Rios is convinced that the Bureau of Indian Affairs in particular and whites in general have crushed Indian families with their care and meddling. Even the trip to Palm Springs was financed by whites—Rios like many Papagos cannot seem to mount a plan of action without first putting his hand out. Still this fact bothers him.

And he is dismayed by what he sees happening in his tribe. Recently at a dance, he noticed a young couple left their baby and two small children in an empty house and drank the night away. Some people tried to find them as the celebration churned around the dance ground but no one did. He thinks this is a bad way to raise kids.

He thinks the whole problem starts this way: the BIA takes the children and sends them to boarding school. They only know their parents as people they visit in the summers, people who usually have no jobs and drink too much. When they get sick, the BIA gives them free medicine. The whole thing seems to lack a center.

His voice is flat as he explores these matters. He has no answers beyond a shrug. He does not even complain. Some things just are. The world spins on and these things happen.

Rios remembers his own days at boarding school. The Bureau sent Indians there to make them more like white people. They came back something else, Indians who had forged friendships with Indians from other tribes, who had created a new identity based on being outsiders in America. Like convicts, they were made over but not the way the system intended.

Now Rios has four children and his marriage has ended. His kids are going through the same childhood he went through with a broken home and boarding schools. He understands this, he accepts this. He does not know what he can do.

A shrug covers a lot of events in the Papago world.

A teenage boy comes in at dawn after spending a wild night. His stepfather empties a .22 into him.

Shrug.

A child kneels and a man feuding with the family blows his head off.

Shrug.

A seventeen-year-old complains about life at the family's kitchen table, walks out drunk, and hangs himself from a mesquite tree.

Shrug.

Rios does not know what he can do. Some things just are.

The next day he picks up his pad of yellow paper and goes downtown to visit the future. The Agua Calientes sit at a long table with passive faces. Here are the fabled Palm Springs Indians, the millionaires who drive Cadillacs. The tribe owns 2,139 acres, mainly mountainside and canyon parks. Individual Agua Calientes own 21,711 acres and much of this ground is Palm Springs. They are considered victors in the centuries-long struggle between native Americans and white people.

Rios and Peter Thomas face them across the huge wooden slab. On the wall blazes a map of the Indians' holdings, a checkerboard pattern with every other section owned by an Agua Caliente.

Barbara Gonzales, a woman of about thirty years, the chairwoman of the Agua Caliente band, sits there like a stock broker. A big diamond sparkles on her hand. Lois Pete, an allottee, has just returned from a vacation in Hawaii with her daughter. She complains of the hotels. Moreno Patencio, twenty-one, has already served as vice chairman, and waits for future shots at power. Another woman sits in with her white financial adviser.

They agree to speak to the Papagos, but not as representatives of the band, solely as individuals dabbling in the local real estate world. This is more than a polite fiction since the Agua Calientes as a people have a tentative existence.

In 1959, after decades of court battles, the band won the right to have its land allotted which meant divided up among the band members as private property. A small morsel was set aside as the tribal holding, but the bulk ceased to belong to the band and passed on to the members. Due to a railroad claim from the nineteenth century, these private holdings were in a checkerboard, one section being Indian, one section non-Indian.

Back in 1959, there were 129 Agua Calientes on the tribal rolls. These people got allotments. Since then band members born into the world can get nothing except by inheritance. Now there are 252 Agua Calientes but many of these people, children born since 1959, own nothing and can only hope to be remembered in a will. Moreno Patencio, for example, owns nothing. A reservation can only be peddled once and the Agua Calientes have sold much of theirs or put it under long-term leases.

This is the history sitting at the table between the Papagos and the Agua Calientes as they talk in the tribe's boardroom. Rios lives in a house without even a cooler. Thomas spends his days cowboying. Barbara Gonzales drives a Saab 900 Turbo, Lois Pete a Lincoln Continental.

In 1883, Helen Hunt Jackson, a famous crusader for Indian rights, described the Agua Calientes this way: "These desert Indians are wretchedly poor and need help perhaps more than any others in Southern California."

In 1961, the *Wall Street Journal* described them again: "Congress recently passed a series of bills which allows the Agua Calientes to divide up about 31,000 acres of high priced tribal land in the center of Palm Springs so each brave, squaw and papoose will have holdings worth at least $335,000. Those who already hold title to lands worth more than that will be allowed to keep such holdings. Some of these holdings are appraised at $1 million."

Today, over the big table Barbara Gonzales cautions the Papagos that it is not that simple. She runs through a patter that sounds much rehearsed, clearly any Agua Caliente worth his or her salt has often had to explain the tribal portfolio and financial picture. Once again, she notes that those born after the great property division have gotten nothing. She points out that some allotments fell in areas that still have not been developed—"as you would say, land rich and cash poor."

Then she turns to Rothschild, a figure of almost demonic potential in Rios' mind.

"He's a businessman, period," she explains smoothly, "a very good businessman and no matter what he says about helping you, he's a businessman."

Patencio tosses in, "Verbal promises don't mean anything."

Gonzales spins right along, "He'll pull you guys apart. He'll see the weak ones and pick them off."

Rios nods.

Soon the room is filled with tales of offers, counteroffers, mistakes, spoiled ventures. The Agua Calientes begin to explode with suspicions. Since 1959, their world has been leases, detailed, mind-numbing, lethal leases. They live on a Monopoly board with about 250 leases and twenty-two percent of the property once in allotments has been sold forever.

Like any good Monopoly board, Palm Springs offers the band members one gut-wrenching terror: you can lose your shirt.

Gonzales notes, "There are a couple in our tribe who may be millionaires. The rest are mainly above median income. Some are at the poverty level, so they have to find jobs."

Today few of the Agua Calientes live in Palm Springs—they are landlords who cannot afford their own rentals. The language is almost gone with only a few old people still speaking it. Gonzales is taking lessons to learn a few words of the dying tongue.

Rios listens and scribbles notes on his big yellow legal pad.

He has lived a different kind of life, one outside the clauses of big leases. One of his brothers is a drunk wandering the towns bordering the reservation in search of that perfect bottle of wine. Rios does not know where he is now—last he heard around Gila Bend.

His life is full of loose, unexplained pieces like his mother. He saw her now and again when he was a kid but was almost a teenager before anyone told him she was his mother. Ask him, why the long deception? and he just shrugs.

On the drive over, he stopped at his sister's house in Casa Grande where family photographs hang over the fireplace, and a bead and feather decoration on one wall echoes the style of Great Plains tribes. In the living room, Rios played a few Spanish runs on the guitar, then a few riffs of rock and roll. His three-year-old niece, "Sexy," squealed across the room. Her father is Walapai, mother Papago, and different family members are teaching her Spanish, Walapi, Papago, and English.

This is the modern American Indian, a kind of conglomerate made out of relationships begun in boarding schools, often a city dweller, often losing a grip on the traditional language and custom and increasingly determined to hold onto the remaining shreds of the past.

Rios, for example, has lived the kind of life where things slip away, and his fierce determination to stop this slide toward nowhere is rooted in bad times.

"I once knew a man," he says, "who knew so many songs and I would ask him to let me tape him." But the old man would not permit such a thing. Rios does not know why. Some things just are.

Then the old man died.

"Cirrhosis of the liver," Rios notes.

Things slip away.

Rios and Thomas are hungry after meeting with the Agua Calientes and try Bob's Big Boy in Palm Springs. The table feels cold with its wood veneer surface and the waitress slams down the silver, tosses huge menus.

The two Papagos search the pages for some scrap of Mexican food and are amazed when it is not there. The room is filled with retired people in sportswear. Thomas wears his huge Stetson with a big plume and cowboy boots.

Rios gives up on the menu and decides to explain a little bit about Papago life. It is a journey toward learning and the learning is what it means to be a Papago. His own education was botched, he feels, because his parents were absent.

"I didn't know," he explains, "how Papagos see things. Take the theory of four—everything comes in four cycles. Even social things have to be in four. They have to be compatible with the four directions. If you don't do it right, everything clashes."

Songs matter also, songs for going to war, songs for coming back, songs for everything encountered in life. His hands rest on the cold table. A cooling unit purrs machine air against his brown skin. He talks on. Songs. Four, cycles of four.

The restaurant is packed. Rios and Thomas are the only human beings in the place with brown skin. They notice this, they always notice this. When they drive around Palm Springs they exclaim over every Mexican they see raking a lawn or carrying out the trash. Their eyes constantly scan the streets looking for the sign of an Indian.

"What I mean," Rios continues, "is when you are here in the

middle of this town—and if I were the only Indian here and if Peter walked in, I would know he was an Indian and that would tell me everything. I wouldn't wonder if he owned a color television, or air conditioning or a credit card. I would know he was an Indian.

"There is a common bond because he is an Indian."

Here he pauses and then says with a smile: "The bond is we all come from Mother Earth."

He pauses again and stares at the tabletop.

"Not," he finishes, "from God."

The food breaks up this lecture. Rios wanted something like a chimichanga. He settles for pancakes and bacon.

"Look," he smiles, "where'd the white people come from? I don't know. You guys claim you came from monkeys."

The white people in the room seem like a foreign culture, all decked out in shorts and bright sport shirts. Their bodies suddenly seem pale, cold, and lacking possibility. They use their forks deftly and chew with their mouths closed. Rios sneaks looks around the room. He is a brown anthropologist making notes on a strange, alien tribe.

"There are certain things you do when you go to the ocean," he suddenly erupts. "Every time I go to the ocean I see people who have driven for miles and they get there and they run in and splash around.

"When I go, I look at it. You have to respect it. You stand there and talk to the water and wait and the water will come to you. But don't just go in and splash around."

There was a time when the Agua Caliente had ideas about the world that could not be captured in the fine print of a lease. One night in 1918 Casimiro showed his power. He was a Cahuilla medicine man—the Agua Caliente were but one band resting in the rich expanse of Cahuilla culture. Casimiro leaped up and tied owl feathers to his head with a band. He grabbed a wooden wand and began to dance around the fire. Soon shaking racked his body and suddenly he plunged the wand down his throat and brought up an object—"out from his heart," according to the explanation—and the shaking ceased.

At other times the power revealed itself in fire-eating. Casimiro would place a hot coal the size of an egg inside his mouth. The people watching him could see the red glow and then he would inhale, blow sparks out his mouth, and finally crush the ember with his teeth, spitting out the ash. Power.

The Agua Caliente, as part of the Cahuilla, belonged to a culture that learned to live with the desert and the mountains. The bands ranged from the hot Mojave up to 10,000-foot peaks blanketed with Douglas fir and pine. They made baskets, gathered seeds, hunted wild game, and healed their weary bones in the hot mineral waters at the place whites later called Palm Springs.

Now the fire-eating has passed and the famous springs are enshrined within a lavish spa. The baskets rest in collections and the Agua Caliente are seldom seen much in the flesh but often discussed by locals as fabulously rich. The Palm Springs Desert Museum dotes on European art but a few scraps of native culture are displayed and some Cahuilla baskets are on exhibit.

There are also Indian books for sale along with Hopi kachinas and Pueblo pots. Two old women handle the cash register in the museum gift shop.

"The Agua Calientes," one explains cheerfully, "mainly left town. They drive around in Cadillacs."

"I used to teach school here," her companion chips in, "and one day I asked the children to tell what their fathers did and one little Indian girl kept silent so I asked her what her father did and she said he didn't do anything. She said, 'Mommy owns all the land over there.' "

The old woman confesses she never forgot that. She says the band used to make beautiful baskets "but now they're rich and they don't have to make anything."

Indian-style pots are offered for sale in the gift shop. They are made by David Salk, a nephew of the polio doctor, Jonas Salk.

Rios and Thomas say nothing.

The next day Moreno Patencio takes them on a grand tour of the area. At the tribal burying ground big beams rest on stone walls and a grader smooths out the lane. Moreno explains that the band is sprucing up the graveyard because developments are planned for the plots adjoining it.

He delivers his insider's view of Palm Springs real estate and points out developments planned or being built by Rothschild. The two Papagos ask him a question.

"Bob Hope?" he responds surprised. "No, I've never seen Bob Hope. This town is pretty expensive—that's why I live down the road ten or fifteen miles. I can't afford to live anywhere near here."

He wheels the Buick Skylark into Cathedral City Country Club, the only Rothschild project actually finished to date. The desert surrenders to lush green lawns and fairways. Condos stud the grounds with soft beige walls. The units go for $100,000 to $130,000 and wear handles like Cypress, Smoketree, Jasmine, and Primrose.

The two Papagos and Moreno waltz into the salesroom where the corporation offers a slick paper booklet with a photo of the old-style Agua Caliente thatched hut on the cover. Under the picture runs the message: MY HOME IS YOUR HOME.

The contents explain "the happy-ending story of Indian leased land in Palm Springs, California." The text extols the financial advantages from leasing Indian land and carefully defuses any frets about dealing with Agua Calientes. Pithy aphorisms sum up the situation:

ONE CANNOT EAT DIRT.

THE ONLY WAY TO BEAT CITY HALL IS TO HAVE THE INDIANS ON YOUR SIDE.

Native American symbols of the sun, the eagle, and the mirage grace the layout.

Moreno paces the living room of the model condo while Rios and Thomas sink into the deep white sofa. The decor is a thick-cushioned fantasy of the Orient. An electric wok waits for an infusion of tofu on the kitchen counter. A bookshelf features two local favorites, *Selling Real Estate Today* and *Real Estate—It's Wonderful*. White walls frame a blue and white tile floor.

Jasmine.

"Glass Window at Entries...Kitchen Nook...Convenient Wet Bar...Domed Skylights for Natural Light in Both Master and Guest Baths...Private Courtyard Entry...Master Bedroom and Living Room Open to Patio With Golf Course or Open Space Views... Clerestory Glass in Both Living and Dining Areas ... Vaulted Ceilings ... Mirrored Wardrobe Doors...Garage Door Opener."

Moreno ignores the room and webs of language spew from his mouth as he paces: ground rents, real estate, percentages, cuts from hotels, residential versus commercial. Rios and Thomas sink deeper into the fat sofa and stare at an Oriental print of distant mountains poking through a mist.

Moreno rolls on, "What's written on paper is what counts. How many Papagos can afford a $127,000 home?"

Rios takes this all in but says nothing. His life has not been cluttered with $127,000 condos.

When he was twenty-one, Rios went to the BIA and said, "Send me away."

They suggested schools in Albuquerque.

"No," he said, "farther."

They offered Tulsa.

"No," he said, "farther."

How about Cleveland?

He went to Cleveland. He felt he had to get out. At San Xavier friends were always dropping by and saying, "Hey, come on, let's go have some fun." At San Xavier, Rios knew he would never stop drinking. So he went to Cleveland and stayed ten years.

For awhile he lived in a slum on $35 a week and went to school. He was lonely and one night he went drinking with a buddy. His friend took the blast from a 16-gauge in the back. Rios remembers the blood dripping down his ripped flesh.

He quit drinking.

His money was tight and sometimes he went hungry. He would get to know other Indians living in the same slums, going to the same schools. One by one, they would slip away and leave no trace. Sometimes he would bump into former classmates on skid row.

For generations, Rios's people had been leaders at San Xavier. In Cleveland, that fact did not count and he spoke Papago with no one. He lived in the snow.

When someone back home would die, he would feel homesick. He'd wish he could be there to put them in the ground.

Moreno moves on into the model kitchen and gives a brief run through of his life. He graduated from high school at fifteen and worked around town. His family has produced band leaders for generations and a street in Palm Springs is named Patencio. So is a business building. His grandfather was the last ceremonial singer and the old man took all his songs to the grave with him.

When Moreno worked as a busboy or dishwasher, he would give a false name.

"Because," he explains, "of the reaction you got. They automatically think you're rich and you don't need to work. They pass you over for promotions."

He plowed through real estate law and became a wizard at reading leases. When the Agua Calientes first came into their big money in 1959, they were patsies. Local lawyers and accountants became the conservators of their holdings—basically their guardians. Many members of the band got fleeced and in the late sixties, the nearby *Riverside Press-Enterprise* won a Pulitzer prize for a series itemizing the scandal.

Moreno itches to renegotiate the early leases. His family now numbers about one hundred. At first the sudden flush of money ripped the group apart, but now he feels they are coming back together. He admits, a little reluctantly, that there are some Agua Calientes hauling in thousands a month, but not that many he quickly adds.

"When I got on the council in 1979," he says, "I contacted the Chamber of Commerce because they were saying we were all rich and that when a child was born, the kid got a million dollars. People don't understand what is going on here. Most of the people in the tribe don't own land and only half those who have land have been able to develop it."

Moreno plans to attend Harvard or Yale if he can line up some scholarship money. Last year he earned $3,000 or $4,000 doing yard work and construction.

He moves the tour along to yet another Cathedral City model condo: The Candlelight. Muzak bathes the room. On the wall is a print of an Oglala Sioux taken in 1840. The old Indian stares grimly ahead, his hand clutching a revolver.

Rios's life does not include plans for Harvard and Yale. When he returned to San Xavier in the early seventies, he was thirty-one and full of fire. He ran for tribal vice chairman and won. Once in office, he started making decisions, a practice almost lethal on the typical reservation, and the decisions made enemies. Rios reentered the traditional Papago world where leaders are distrusted as soon as they are selected and quick decisions considered an affront to the true nature of things. He ran for chairman twice and lost twice.

In the eyes of many of his fellow tribal members, he had lost his Papago essence.

Now he swears he is finished with politics, a statement about as believable from an Indian politico as from an Anglo one. But he does wear the scars of his campaigns in his eyes. They are weary and hurt. Four times he has been shot at and for a while he packed a gun.

Enough, he insists. He will tend to his own interests. But this new development plan with the intricate lease has hauled him out of his would-be retirement. The old instincts have revived.

Rios is a man of constant motion and energy. He travels with a loose-leaf binder stuffed with telephone numbers. He knows Arizona Senator Dennis DeConcini and once worked for him. He knows Governor Bruce Babbitt and has delivered Papago votes on election day. He serves on national Indian boards and jets off to Central America, Las Vegas, and Hawaii to hobnob with other members of a red network.

But he is still a Papago. His truck seized up months ago and lies dead in his yard. He lives in a home without a telephone and to know him one must be part chauffeur and part answering service.

He says he is only in this land thing to protect his children's future inheritance. But that is not what his eyes say.

He stalks Palm Springs greedy for any tidbit of information. He scrutinizes the brilliant green golf courses with disbelief, and he notes such oddments as a Rolls-Royce dealership.

And then he scribbles more notes on his long legal pad.

The pre-Palm Springs and pre-lavish resort Agua Caliente band believed in a world of chance, a place created in part as the result of indecision and mistakes. The old language captured this tentative feel of things. Simple concrete facts were often framed by expressions like "I guess" or "maybe so." Perhaps, this world view has helped them understand why rich people have descended on their dry desert near the ancient springs.

Moreno Patencio speaks no Cahuilla. He is a modern man, born after the settlement of 1959, a man who has never known anything but Palm Springs as a resort. He looks forward, believes progress is inevitable and just wants to make sure his tribe gets its share of the spoils.

He keeps bombarding Rios and Thomas with tips on negotiating leases.

"Just signing a lease won't do it," he cautions. "That's going to cause the downfall of a tribe. You have to prepare for the day the property reverts back to you."

He drives the Buick down streets lined with condos, golf courses, and sheltered estates. For Thomas and Rios all this hip real estate talk is a bit of a fantasy. They, too, are well mired in modern life and like its treats and luxuries. But they are constantly drifting backward, spinning out of prescribed orbits to attend Papago dances that go on until dawn in some empty flat of desert, wild revels where mesquite smoke floats across the assembled and nobody is likely to make it to work the next day.

Suddenly, Moreno pulls up by a huge vacant parcel. This, he tells Rios, is one of Rothschild's leases. Burro weed and creosote carpet the sand. A wind from the west sings across the emptiness. Rios snaps pictures of the undeveloped ground.

Then he walks off into the landscape, bends here and there plucking at plants, and returns with clippings of things he knows back home. He shows them to Moreno and asks him if his people use them also.

Moreno says the old ones sometimes know such things.

That night the road rolls under the headlights as Rios continues to prowl the Palm Springs area. Peter curls up in back with a can of Coors and the comfort of chicken scratch music. Rios slouches deep into the front seat, his face frozen, his voice barely audible. As he speaks, he stares forward as if he were talking to no one at all.

He keeps returning to Cleveland. It was a good thing for him, he says. He saw things there, he proved he could make it in the white world, and he quit the bottle.

One night, he remembers, he left his room, a cheap flop on a bad street, and he started down the fire escape when he heard a noise. A woman was screaming.

He looked down and saw half a dozen guys lined up and gang-raping a woman. He was afraid they would hear him and take him out, so he simply froze. They stood there patiently in line and had her one by one.

But what he remembers most is not the men having their way with the woman. His memory is stuck on the way they walked away afterwards.

He says they did not even hurry, they just ambled off as if nothing had happened, nothing at all.

The green glow off the dashboard plays across his face.

The following day brings a power lunch. Men and women stretch out in rows by a blue pool. They are fat and now they want to be fat and tan. The men drink, smoke and talk. The women tend to lie on their bellies, halter straps untied, and bronze. The sun carefully roasts them in the patio of the Sheraton Plaza in Palm Springs. Barbara Gonzales, Moreno Patencio, Mike Rios, and Peter Thomas are seated in the glass-walled dining room off the pool area. A noon-time fashion show parades past the table offering young women in swim suits with large breasts and steady smiles. The Indians ignore the trim young women modeling and the fat people sunning. They talk business.

The Sheraton rests on Indian-owned land. It is the kind of place favored by the city fathers of Palm Springs. K-Marts, Safeways, Gemcos, and the like have been kept out of the city: the wrong tone. The Sheraton has the right tone.

Lunch runs ten bucks a throw.

Rios asks the waiter what they have to drink.

"Anything you want," he sniffs.

Rios asks for root beer, the waiter retreats defeated. The models continue to prowl and their flesh looks delicious amid the clutter of tables, the fat patrons spilling out of swim suits and sport shirts.

Moreno cranks up another talk on leases. He says the lease on the original spa at Palm Springs will be up in eighty-nine years, and he intends to be around to renegotiate the terms. His words come out like paper ribbon off a ticker tape.

The models with their breasts swimming over their halter tops, with their hard abdomens, do not make him skip a beat. The man is locked into his eighty-nine-year mission.

Lunch ends finally and the Agua Calientes spring for the check.

On the way out of town, Rios insists on pulling off at a gas station. He disappears into the restroom and comes out innocent of his slacks and dress shirt. He is back to faded Levis and boots.

Thomas slaps another chicken scratch tape, one by the Papago Raiders, into the cassette player. Rios stuffs all his notes into an attaché case and snaps the lid shut.

He laughs on the drive back. And keeps going over that lease.

Her hands are small and so are her wrists and she curls on the sofa like a cat, her quick eyes flickering off every word or move. There has been a sex crime and I have come to drain her of this experience. But she is not ready to go into that matter just yet. Before the talk can come, she must tell me who she is and this cannot be accomplished by flashing a class ring, showing me her car, or discussing favorite restaurants.

She lights a cigarette, the fingers long and slender and now the voice begins, rough but very low.

She talks of her grandmother and her father. As she speaks of them she becomes seven years old.

The voice commands attention as it heads into the past.

Her grandmother says please don't go; her father says he has to make a living and the seven-year-old child watches. He leaves for his job on an oil rig in the Gulf of Mexico. The old woman drops her plea, does not tell him of her dream. Dreams never quite make sense in the morning.

In this one, the old woman sees the man is driving down the highway when suddenly the road opens up and he falls into a black pit. The old woman focuses her will and with her mind pulls him back up the other side. That is the first part of the dream she does not tell the man.

Of course, for the man the dream does not exist at all. He goes to his job on the oil rig out in the Gulf. There is an old deaf-mute there who carries water for the crew. They chip in a few bucks a week for his pay.

This morning a crane dangles a huge pipe by two chains. One chain snaps and the pipe begins to twirl like a blade. The men run except for the old deaf-mute who hears nothing. He walks toward the pipe twirling lower and lower over his head. The man who was in the old woman's dream sees the mute and goes back for him. He grabs him and pitches him aside like a sack of laundry. The old mute lands clear and safe on the cool deck over the warm Gulf.

In the old woman's dream, her son continues down the road after escaping the pit when suddenly a second pit opens up. He stops before the hole and then drives down into it. The old woman focuses all her will on her son down in that hole and after a spell, the car comes chugging up the other side and he is still at the wheel.

Out on the oil rig in the Gulf, the pipe cuts across both his hips smashing them to pulp and he goes down hard on the deck. His hands are still over his head from pitching the deaf-mute and he cannot break his fall. A six-inch spike punches between his eyes. He lies there and then slowly pulls himself off it. The other men rush over.

He says, "Don't call my wife. I have to talk to her or she'll get upset."

In the old woman's dream her son drives on without a care when a third hole opens up. The car pauses and then rolls down and this time the old woman can do nothing.

At the hospital, a coma swallows the man from the oil rig and doctors say he recognizes nothing, knows nothing. His wife stands by his bed, her long black hair hanging. When he would come home from the oil rig, he delighted in brushing that long black hair. Now he reaches out from his bed, from the tubes feeding his body, and touches his wife's hair.

On the third day, the doctors say he will never have control of his mind again. The man squeezes his wife's hand and is gone.

The woman on the sofa finishes her story. She is no longer seven. Her grandmother is long dead. But this is not her past, this is her present—the morning of the dream is a message whispering in her blood.

She takes a drag on her cigarette and the smoke drips from her red lips. She does not say what the story means or why she has brought it up before discussing the sex crime.

Her eyes no longer dart but look long and hard and clear. She is ready to talk of the other matter and the story will take eighteen hours. That will be no problem. Now she has told me who she is.

Foreman

I've always done those things. Anytime I see a
sign or a fucking survey stake that shouldn't
be there, I fuck with it. I fuck with machines
too.

> —Doug Peacock,
> AKA George Washington Hayduke
> of *The Monkey Wrench Gang*,
> on decorum in the wilds.

THE FIFTH OF DARK BACARDI RUM waits on the car roof as Dave
Foreman changes into camouflage shorts, shirt, and hat. His pale
beer-swollen belly braves the rays of the Colorado Plateau.

This is the morning after. Foreman and his two friends are coming
off the twentieth anniversary of the death of Glen Canyon, a doom
dated from the day in 1963 when the penstocks on the dam closed
and the Colorado River began to swallow 107 canyons, 10,000 Anasazi
sites, and a stretch of water John Wesley Powell in his passage of 1871
named after the glens of trees. Interior Secretary James Watt came
for the hoopla, the Del Webb Corporation dedicated some new hotel
rooms and a couple of tour boats at the marina and the governors of
Utah and Arizona joined in the merry-making. Earth First!, a group
Foreman helped spawn, held a requiem.

87

Foreman winces in the light. His blond hair and beard toss in the breeze. For days while he talked wilderness, the small herd of ecological misfits struggled to relight a fire snuffed somewhere around 1969. At Lake Powell, the Earth Firsters! had been magic and energy. I had felt myself being seduced by pleasures abandoned years before.

Now Foreman and his companions throw down some Bacardi courage and walk into the real wilderness. They do not want to talk to a newspaper now. After the loud words of the requiem, they tackle the stone of the plateau. Wire Pass chokes on a boulder and a six-foot drop leads to the cool sands. The red walls leap up a hundred feet, the body must turn sideways to fit through the passage. The slit is cool and dark and the sky becomes a cobalt thread high overhead. Logs jammed far above mark the reach of the flood waters. This is a sure place to die in the cloudbursts of summer.

The slit enters sunlight at Buckskin Gulch where Anasazi petroglyphs pecked in the stone remember a dozen bighorn sheep. Then the narrowness returns and the channel becomes a ten-mile slit dubbed the Dive of the Buckskin with 400-foot walls.

One man goes ahead. Foreman and the woman straggle along. Cool air chills the skin, swallows dart five hundred feet above, combs of wild bees hang from the red rock, and talk bounces off the walls.

The woman climbs into a small grotto and has a snack. Foreman leans against the stone slab. His voice is low and mumbling. He has fed the media for days and now the words need a rest.

Time was there for the birthday and *Newsweek, U.S. News and World Report,* the *Philadelphia Inquirer, Los Angeles Times, Rocky Mountain News* out of Denver, NBC television, ZDF (West German National TV), Associated Press, U.P.I., and papers from Arizona and Utah. They came for the magic confrontation between Secretary of Interior James Watt and Earth First!, the weird ones of the American environmental movement. The press feasted on a pirate ship, Beach Boy tunes, t-shirts that suggested SAVE A COYOTE/POISON A SHEEP-MAN, the image of a monkey wrench crossed with a tomahawk. I filed dutifully once or twice a day, wore a t-shirt that said FUCK BECHTEL and greeted Secretary Watt with a lapel pin designating me the widow of a retired Methodist minister. There was something in the air that violated logic and I sucked it deep into my lungs.

The story played like this: a small group wants to tear down Glen Canyon Dam and rants for more wilderness, more canyons, more mountains, more trees, swamps, plagues, and pestilences. The assorted governors, bureaucrats, and Secretary Watt offer a backdrop of reason. Little that I wrote saw print and the editors were not amused. Then after a few days it was over, the media and the politicos packed up, and the canyon was left to its watery grave.

Foreman and some of his troops retreated into the plateau to relax as did I and in the dive of the Buckskin we stumbled into each other. High above the rock walls a jetliner traces a trail across the sky.

No place is wild enough anymore.

Foreman thinks about the question. It is Thursday, the day of Watt's visit, and he looks like a hangover wearing a black Earth First! t-shirt, jeans, Puma running shoes. He hunkers like a bear.

"Glen Canyon Dam," he finally allows, "is a big mother and nothing less than a small nuclear weapon can take the sucker out."

He pauses and delivers up the punch line: "the Libyans have yet to respond."

Down by the shore of Lake Powell, the crew loads the pirate ship, a 50-foot houseboat rented from the Del Webb Corporation. A mannequin of James Watt decked out in a nice suit and sunglasses kneels on the sand in a prayerful attitude with arms raised to the heavens. A Coors can is clutched in the right hand.

A couple of miles west along the beach sits the big white plug, the 710-foot dam fat with 4,901,000 cubic yards of concrete, tense with the pressure of two years' flow of the Colorado at its back, mighty with 1,124,000 kilowatts of power spewing from its loins on those record-beating days when everything in the watershed clicks. At the base the dam is 600 feet thick and deep in its bowels plumb lines track its shudders from the drive of the trapped river yearning for the sea.

The electric juice sizzles out to communities in Arizona, Colorado, Utah, Wyoming, New Mexico, and Nebraska. On hot days it cools Phoenix; on cold days it warms Salt Lake City. Many of the dam's original proponents now say they have regrets—men like former Interior Secretary Stewart Udall, former head of the Sierra Club

David Brower, and Arizona Senator Barry Goldwater. They now say, never again.

Earth First! says "Crack Glen Canyon Dam."

At the group's campsite, Ken Sanders' belly spills over his shorts and he needs help. The ambulance arrives just in time. It is part of the forces of surveillance, teams of security that dog the steps of Earth First! at Glen Canyon Dam. Sanders walks over and begins talking with the three ambulance attendants who have been dispatched to monitor the eco-hordes for three days and nights. They are part of a warrior shield featuring the Arizona Highway Patrol, Utah Highway Patrol, National Park Service police, assorted county sheriffs, Secret Service agents, and bodyguards brought by the governors of Arizona and Utah and the Secretary of the Interior. Squad cars watch the small encampment at Lone Rock from the hills. Today, eight Earth Firsters! must suffice to represent the awful environmental threat. Bart Koehler, AKA Johnny Sagebrush, the bard of Earth First's! music, paddles out to the ambulance.

He asks for some Rolaids and grapples with a can of Blatz.

Sanders compliments the attendants on providing a handy pharmacy for the camp. He is an environmental media man, putting out annual calendars and a line of books printed under imprint of Dream Garden Press. He operates out of Salt Lake City and in his veins runs the blood of one of Mormonism's founding families.

A large part of Earth First's! identity comes from print. The scattered chapters in the organization operate autonomously and a newspaper published from time to time provides the most frequent common ground. The publication thunders with warnings like this: "Agent provocateurs will be dealt with by the Grizzly Defense League on the Mirror Plateau."

Today, Sanders is at liberty from the pressures of deadlines and proofreading. He drinks a beer and helps unload a coffin that will symbolize Glen Canyon and a headstone for the grave.

He explains, "Glen Canyon Dam is the world's largest tombstone and Lake Powell is the world's largest cemetery—it's where the drowned things are."

His hair hangs in a ponytail, his beard sweeps down in a patriarchal expanse, and his head buzzes from the firewater guzzled

the night before at the Water Dog Saloon in nearby Glen Canyon
City.

The assembled eco-warriors make their first high strategy decision
for the day: they won't get wasted again tonight. Apparently, this is
not an easy goal to achieve. At hand is Secretary Watt, a person who
has become the demon of the environmental movement. Johnny
Sagebrush has immortalized the man in a song.

Tune: "Will the Circle Be Unbroken"

Well, I saw a Black Cloud coming
It was coming from the East
Riding like a swirling monster
Was a bureaucratic beast.

The beast himself looks relaxed down at a nearby resort. The
Stetson sits square on his head, the suit is wrinkle-free and a giant
bolo tie fashioned from petrified wood and green gemstone perches
on his neck. On the lapel, a gold pin announces WYOMING.

Secretary James Watt has arrived for lunch at the Rainbow Room
of the Wahweap Lodge. He is a cheerful man and moves with ease
and without pretense through the crowd of diners. A smile comes
naturally to his face. Here is the demon and he is impossible to
dislike. I think I should ask him a question and then realize I have
nothing to ask.

He talks to anyone and he speaks his mind clearly and bluntly. He
has said heretical things: the Grand Canyon is a bore. Indian Reser-
vations are socialist enclaves. For these and other utterances, he is
periodically woodshedded in Washington and flogged daily in the
press. But he is attractive simply because he is a terrible player in
the political wars. Watt is the last thing anyone expects from a Cabi-
net member—honest, plain, and friendly. If he and Foreman dined
together, I can't help but think they would probably chuckle over
each other's remarks.

Of course, that is not in the script. Watt must play his role as
demon and Earth First! must represent the lunatic fringe threaten-
ing the peace and quiet of the Republic. Outside on the lodge

grounds, swarms of security men mumble into walkie-talkies and poke through trash bins searching for the magic bombs of the environmental guerrillas.

Tune: "When The Saints Go Marching In"

When the sky begins to fall
When the sky begins to fall
Hot damn I want to be in that number
That puts Watt up against the wall.

Foreman and Koehler once wore suits and ties and worked for the Wilderness Society as field representatives and Washington, D.C. lobbyists. Foreman, raised in New Mexico, was the head of the state's far-right Young Americans for Freedom during college, toyed with the idea of becoming a minister, and in the late sixties volunteered for the Marine Corps so he could go to Vietnam and defend the nation from godless communism. He spent half his brief stint in the brig and was pitched out as unfit for the Corps. His flaw: he would not obey orders.

Then came the Wilderness Society and then came the moment when something snapped. Koehler and Foreman threw over their budding bureaucratic careers, wandered down into Mexico, trekked through the volcanic wilderness of the Pinacate, and over a beer in San Luis, Sonora, conjured up Earth First! They decided the environmental organizations had become too tame and were kept pets of the federal agencies, so they created an anarchistic organization that would be too disorderly to penetrate and too extreme to be swallowed.

Earth First! ventured forth as a new American theater group. They hiked into the Gila Wilderness of New Mexico and erected a monument to Victorio, an Apache chief relentless in his resistance to settlement. Earth First! unrolled a cellophane crack down the face of Glen Canyon Dam as a signal of a better future. All over the West, little chapters began blocking logging roads, monkey-wrenching mineral exploration efforts, fighting the destruction of remaining tracts of wilderness. And going to jail for their actions.

In part, the group is a product of Edward Abbey's *The Monkey*

Wrench Gang, a novel about destroying the things that destroy the West, especially Glen Canyon Dam. And partly, it flows from a new perception about how human beings and wild ground should coexist, a school of thought called Deep Ecology.

The group's manifesto says, "We are emotional, passionate and angry. We also have a sense of humor....We say the ideas of Western Civilization are anti-earth, anti-woman, and anti-liberty. We are working to develop a new biocentric paradigm: Deep Ecology."

The members tend to be over thirty, to hold down odd jobs, or do seasonal work for the Forest Service and Park Service.

Now they are busy loading the pirate ship for James Watt. A black flag complete with skull and crossbones flutters in the breeze. The mannequin clutching the Coors kneels on the prow. The ship is the first vessel in the Lake Foul Navy, a force dedicated to scuttling houseboats and sinking the highpower craft dragging water skiers.

The crew is varied. The man dressed as a pirate is an actor from Sante Fe. Stacy, blonde and busy flashing her long eyelashes, sips a Budweiser. She's been in Earth First! about a month and in between the fire fights of the eco-wars, she is a travel agent. Her boyfriend is too sloshed for much chat now. He is a student of every Bureau of Land Management trick in western Utah and this seems to constitute his work.

Men and women and children scramble over the pirate ship decking out the sides with signs, dummies, and doodads. Then the pirate ship pulls out into the lake.

Tune: "Were You There When They Crucified My Lord?"

Spirit come and tear this dam away
Spirit come and tear this dam away
Oh, sometimes it causes me to tremble, tremble
Spirit come and blow this dam away.

The official ceremonies must buck the natural weather. Storm lashes the lake and the governors of Arizona and Utah stand with their wives on a heaving dock beside the two new tour boats. The Page Arizona High School Band bleats on the shore as cold drops fall. Governor Babbitt of Arizona conjures up the ghost of John Wesley

Powell in his remarks and looks pained when the Earth Firsters! on
shore chant "Nuke Watt." The pirate ship cruises nearby with
women dancing on the top deck and screams of savage pleasure
pouring from the crew. A police craft monitors the Lake Foul Navy
like a pilot fish keeping pace with a shark. A boat full of press rocks in
the waves and the cameras whirr away.

Then the governors' ladies burst champagne bottles on the new
boats, the rain comes down heavily, and phase one of the Del Webb
Lake Powell party soaks to an end. A man on shore shoulders a
placard, ANASAZIS AGAINST WATT. Moments later the Earth First!
Air Force whines into view as a one-engine plane drags a banner,
EF!—FREE THE COLORADO.

The gods of the Colorado Plateau whip up a four-foot chop on the
lake.

Tune: "Rollin' In My Sweet Baby's Arms"

Well, you can't screw around with Mother Nature
You can't screw around with that old girl
You can't screw around with Mother Nature anymore
'Cause she's coming to take back her world.

After the blessing of the tour boats, Earth First! regroups for a
rally. Ken Sleight stands on the tailgate of a truck and tells the crowd
that Glen Canyon water was good for washing, skinny dipping, and
making love. He is over fifty, gray-haired, and he ran this stretch of
the river for years before the dam stopped the fun. Abbey based
Seldom Seen Smith of the *The Monkey Wrench Gang* on Sleight's
lank frame and loving habits.

The Earth First! event sputters along at the official Fish Cleaning
Station. They have been banished from the nearby Wahweap Lodge,
lest they ruin a banquet for Watt. There the Secretary dines on beef
stroganoff and tells the audience that he has saved the national parks
from ruin by adding handrails at Bryce Canyon and getting the Children's Nature School rewired at Zion. He also declares his fondness
for Lake Powell and pride in the big dam. He is at ease with the
crowd and when the press pitches him some barbed questions, he
devours them like a wolf in a sheep pen. And always, always, he
offers that serene smile.

Out under the gray skies, Sleight rattles on with his love of the
river that is now buried at his back. He reads from a poem by a
friend,

> They dream of a mighty boom and a quake
> They dream of a river wild and free
> Freed from its shackles by TNT.

At this juncture Earth Last! descends and interrupts the speech-
making. The Earth Lasters!, a lunatic fringe of the Earth First's!
lunatic fringe, breaks up all such gatherings in the hope that such
efforts will keep the faithful from becoming self-righteous humbugs.
The Earth Last! folk come on three-wheeled ATCs and dressed as
smokestacks. A heap of naked mannequins holds a placard stating
MUTANTS FOR WATT. An Earth Last! speaker reveals that Watt does
not have sex with animals, that Ronald Reagan is the Fuhrer Christ of
the Aquarian Age and concludes, "Progress First, People Second,
Earth Last."

> *Bart Kohler is also my best friend and the only*
> *person I know who is more full of shit than*
> *I am.*
>   —Dave Foreman, *Lil' Green Songbook*

Foreman ambles up like a shy bear. The shoulders slope down, the
chest leans forward, the arms come up like logs seeking to embrace
the Earth Firsters! Foreman stands in the center of the Fish Cleaning Station and unleashes thunder.

The mumble is gone now, the voice comes out a hoarse, rasping
weapon. He is an endangered species all to himself: the American
stump speaker.

"We had a wonderful Earth First! float trip down the Grand Canyon," the voice begins. "The only problem we had was getting our
forty-two cases of beer through Crystal Rapids, and we decided to
drink it before we got to Lava Falls."

While they were quaffing the beer a Park Service group arrived.
Foreman noticed "this obnoxious guy. He was funny looking, bald-
headed, and wore glasses." The man demanded a helicopter to take
him out of the Canyon.

"All of a sudden," Foreman reveals, "I realized who he was and I jumped up and said, 'You're Jim Watt!' And everybody on the beach jumped up too. And I said, 'Stick where you are! Leave him to me! He's my meat!'

"I threw my hat off and said you lay there till the carnage is settled. I threw off my life jacket and said you lay there till his suffering's done.

"'Hooeeeee! I'm the bloodiest son of a wildcat that lives! I'm going to eat you for lunch, you half-human land raper. Why I'm the old original half-grizzly, half-wolf, half-rattlesnake from the Wild West.

"'I'm the man they call Summer Thunder and Sundance. Why I'm sired by a hurricane, dammed by an earthquake, half-brother to the cholera, nearly related to the smallpox on my mother's side.

"'Why I take seventeen Bechtel executives and a barrel of whiskey for breakfast when I'm in robust health and a bushel of dirt bikers and a damn bulldozer when I'm not.

"'I'll split Glen Canyon Dam with my glance, and the blood of oil executives is my natural drink.

"'So cast your eye on me you half-human, land-raping, anti-environmentalist scumbag, for I'm about to eat you for lunch.'

"Well, I figured after that old Jim Watt would fly right out of the Grand Canyon without that helicopter. You can imagine how surprised I was when he jumped up and said, 'Hoooeeee! Cast your eye on me and pray you environmentalist extremist, perfect child of environmental calamity, for I'll eat you for lunch. Hold me down to earth sweet Jesus for I feel my powers a working. Don't attempt to look at me with the naked eye. When I'm in a playful mood, I use the meridians of latitude and the parallels of longitude for a seine as I drag the Pacific Ocean for whales. When I'm thirsty, I suck the Colorado dry. When I'm hot, I dam the rivers of the West to air condition the desert. When I'm cold, I boil San Francisco Bay with radioactive wastes.

"'The destruction of endangered species is the pastime of my idle moments and the devastation of whole ecosystems is the serious business of my life. The industrial wasteland is my enclosed property and I'll bury my dead on my own premises.

"'So cast your eye on me you environmental extremist for the kingdom of industrialism is going to eat you for lunch.'"

Here Foreman pauses in his thunder and surveys the crowd.

"Well," he resumes more softly, "what that encounter proved to me is that rhetoric is not enough....

"What we've got to do is recognize the wilderness and the preservation of natural diversity as a moral issue, as an ethical issue. It's not a question of different lifestyles or recreation opportunities. It's a moral issue....

"Glen Canyon has a right to exist for its own sake; the wilderness is the real world, it's where we come from, it's life, it's our mother....

"It's time to stop talking about parts per billion, about acres in National Parks. It's time to make it a moral issue.

"And if we do that and we go the next step and be visionaries and we don't just respond to what they give us then we don't just comment on the Bureau of Land Management wilderness review.

"We have the vision, we have the daring to say tear down Glen Canyon Dam. Let the Sierra Club be afraid to say tear down dams. But we can do it and we will see Glen Canyon alive and free, flowing and green in our lifetimes because we can do *what we will to do.*

"The other thing is we've got the ethic, we've got the vision, we can have the courage, the courage of Gandhi, the courage of Martin Luther King, to put our bodies between what we love and the agents of destruction."

Foreman finishes as he began, standing in a small circle of people under a gray sky, the wind smothering his words as it rips across the Colorado Plateau.

Over at the Lodge, Foreman's talk does not touch the work at hand. A bomb dog sniffs for explosives.

"Seek, Dutch, seek," his handler begs.

Dutch works his nose around and finds nothing. Should he ever stumble upon any nukes, artillery shells, dynamite, landmines, explosive plastique or gunpowder, he will instantly sit down. That is how he is trained.

Watt sits safe inside at a table of the Rainbow Room wolfing down his supper and watching a Navajo do a hoop dance.

The Secretary's day is about over. He missed Foreman's speech and confessed to hardly noticing any protestors. The next day he will tour some of the parks in southern Utah. For him Glen Canyon Dam and Lake Powell are not issues. They are a generating facility and a reservoir.

Back at the Earth First! encampment the day ends differently.

People sing "Twist and Shout," "Time Is On Our Side," "Heart of Stone." They whip through fifties classics, folk tunes, forgotten chartbusters. The bonfire leaps high and a night chill falls on the beach of Lone Rock campground. Police still watch the Earth Firsters! from the hillside.

Watt turns out not to be a demon. The environmental crazies turn out not to toss bombs. And the slow degradation of the West continues, the growing numbers of humans, machines, power plants, dams, roads, thirsts, bellies, and fangs.

If anything has changed, it is out at Lone Rock where people sing and laugh like, well, like it was still 1968. There are only a couple thousand members of Earth First! and fewer than one hundred here.

It does not seem like much when you add it up.

But it sounds like much more.

There is a hint of promise in the air.

Of course, that was all days ago and now the singing has stopped and stone demands silence.

A short way down Buckskin Gulch past the grotto where Foreman and the woman pause and relax, an owl blocks the narrow canyon. The bird is big and has no visible wounds. Some sickness perhaps has dragged him down into this chute 400 feet high and 10 feet wide.

The bird puffs up and spreads his wings, rocks defiantly from foot to foot. He is afraid and this is his best bluff. He is willing to defend his ground.

He clacks his beak again and again and the sound echos off the rock. He will probably die here. The walls soar hundreds of feet through worlds laid down millions of years ago. The owl, Foreman, the woman, the daylight seeping over the rim against the upper lip of the gulch—all these things are just a footnote to one more day.

This is a wild place.

The woman puts a match to a Kool Light and the smoke rises idly toward the acoustical tile ceiling. There are no windows, the street lies nine floors below. Crime victims come here to try and fix the wounds in their minds.

The woman wears brown slacks, her eyes are very clear, and the voice flows smoothly and with confidence. The cigarette sits like a delicate wand between her fingers. We are wrangling over how names will be handled in a story. She is very insistent that her clients' identities be kept secret and safe. An industrial vacuum cleaner opens up with a roar in the hallway and the woman speaks through the sound without a pause.

Then the noise of the vacuum cleaner is ripped open by another woman's voice coming through the wall from a nearby room. This new voice does not sound too old and the words tumble out powered by little bursts of hysteria.

The voice shrieks that he came in through the window and I was in the bathroom and he made me take off my clothes.

The vacuum cleaner is relentless in its quest for dirt. The machine roar rises and falls, sometimes smothering the voice, sometimes not. The voice cannot seem to stop its account. He told me to turn around. He told me to bend over.

The voice says, "I feel so dirty."

The woman sitting in her ninth-floor office without windows continues calmly explaining her concerns. Smoke rolls from her mouth.

"Is that voice on a tape?" I ask.

"No," she replies.

Company Man

HE DRINKS STRAIGHT SHOTS in the pink bar filled with laughing people. The women look warm and friendly, the men shoot pool and talk out the day's work. On the wall, trophies from dune-buggy races recall the outside world.

Ajo plunges into another night and the middle-aged man is protective of Ajo. He snarls and spits bitter words at me. He has decades invested in the place and resentments spill from him about press stories, television stories, reporters, editors, headlines. I sip my beer and wait for the cloud of anger to pass. I have had this moment before when the patient dying on the table suddenly wants the room cleared of spectators. Ajo is mortally wounded and for months I have been dropping in on the deathbed and then leaving again for the outside world.

The small copper town 50 miles from the Mexican line and 140 miles west of Tucson is living out a bad dream. For decades no one seemed to leave and generations piled up on top of one another. In a nation where the average family packs their bags every five years, Ajo sons followed their fathers and grandfathers into the pit. Ajo became a kind of stable island in a world of drift and motion.

Then came a layoff that stretched almost a year, followed by a few months' work. In July 1983 the old contract ended and a strike was called as was the custom. But for the first time, the company did not simply shut down while new terms were hammered out. Instead, the company replaced the strikers with new hires—scabs to the strikers—and the town that in the past few people had left suddenly saw new faces arrive and old faces pitched into exile. One brother might cross the line for a job, one brother might not. The thick hide that was two, three, four generations deep cracked like an eggshell.

In the press, the strike was periodic violence and a constant drone about cost-of-living adjustment, medical benefits, and wages. The town, and other Arizona copper camps, would be left for days or weeks in the doldrums of the strike and then suddenly leap to the front page for shootings, window bashings, and demonstrations. A small girl took a slug through the head but survived unimpaired. Little bundles of rhetoric between union and company negotiators would come and go on the back pages. The core of Ajo slowly evolved into a thing no one had expected or looked for. The strike seemed almost out of sight in the town but always present—like an ice pick buried in the brain.

I am not a union man. I am not the man who joins things. I am not a company man. I am not the man who ever believes in the corporation. And I am not neutral. When I was a boy, my old man would rail against the unions, sketch them as the opening gun of a collectivist society. Of course, he railed against the corporations, trusting nothing much larger than family and blood. And when I was seven, my uncle, on strike at a refinery, took me down to the union hall. I remember sitting there perched on a stool while the men drained long necks and talked strategy. They were going to blow up a man's house. And I suspect they did.

So I come to this town with this baggage and for months have watched two tired giants, the union and the corporation, act out a death dance a long time coming.

The place once had maybe 5,000 people and now no one really knows but the guess is around 4,500 or 3,500—and falling. The people are angry and dulled by the long drag of the struggle. Both sides are armed and yet very little happens. The men go to separate bars, the homes of non-strikers and strikers sit side by side and somehow the families coexist. The children meet at the schools and do not talk of their fathers' work or lack of work. The sun shines almost every day of the year and when you come to town you see the sun and the little company houses and hardly ever the strike.

The man in the Hot L bar looks across at me and his eyes drip contempt. Amid the general laughter, he buys me drinks and keeps up with insults, complaints, and scorn. He wants to talk but first he must establish his lack of need for talk. Sugar, the bar dog, stares in from the doorway, tail wagging, and her beagle eyes dream of a handout.

Finally, the man snorts, "You want to know Ajo? I'll show you Ajo."

His car is a Lincoln Continental, new, long, and full of buttons beckoning power. He has given his life to Phelps Dodge, the copper company, and he has been paid. He rolls slowly down the dark streets talking Ajo, Ajo, Ajo.

He wants to get things down right. He knows most people don't give a damn about Ajo, don't even know where it is and if they do, they write the place off as a miserable company town. Most people don't matter to him. Ajo does. The place is by some measurements 130 years old and then July 1 the strike came and new hires and families split. People left and people came.

"That's academic," the man snarls, "I'll show you the real Ajo. History? Sociology? To hell with them."

He is half drunk and the big car rolls into the darkness of the town.

The first miners came in 1854 and Ajo ore was packed down to Guaymas in Sonora and shipped around the Horn to Wales for smelting. The second shipload sank at sea and there the venture ended.

The old man came to the Gila River country in 1848 and lived on beans, corn, dried fruit, and wild game, just like the Indians. He moved to Ajo in 1884 and brought along his son, Tom Childs, Jr., born in Yuma in 1870. The old man and the boy worked the abandoned diggings. The boy took to the place, a hard desert with nine inches of rain at one end and three inches at the other. He ran with the Sand Papagos, small bands totaling maybe two or three hundred people in all, who roamed the wild country to the west.

The boy became a man and married several Sand Papago women. He ate what they ate. The large army worms were a bother.

"Those legs are still very sticky and thorny," he found, "and would always stick in my throat."

Ajo slept; Tom Childs, Jr., roared.

Until the strike, The Hut was a solid union bar. Then new owners bought it and now anyone can theoretically drink here. Tonight when the company man and I enter, two people drink in the huge room. The dance floor lies in darkness—once Cesar Chavez spoke to a screaming strike crowd here about *huelga*, solidarity, the cause. He was a small brown man with a flat voice and his words were clichés. This did not matter. He was a Mexican who had refused to take it anymore and the audience glowed with his presence. All sign of that day has vanished.

The two guys at the bar sip rum and cokes.

Bagdad, a mining camp in the north of Arizona, went under, one explains, "and this is all I ever heard back on after sending out fifty resumes."

He is twenty-seven and slumps under his big cowboy hat. At the mine in Bagdad he made $11 an hour. Here he draws $7, the basic wage for the new non-union employees. Wages since the strike began have been slashed for new hires—the company is being crushed by sinking copper prices and argues such economies are a necessity. The man from Bagdad has never belonged to a union. He and his friend have been in Ajo a week and they live in PD's dormitory.

The company man talks to the woman bartender and asks about family. One guy from Bagdad gets up from his stool and throws a buck into the jukebox. He is lanky and hungry. The plump Mexican woman tending the bar smiles. They dance, slow and close. The house lights are almost off and they spin in darkness.

The man with the big cowboy hat does not know much about the strike. He finds the shift change an aggravation because the handful of strikers on the picket line shout "Scab."

What does he think when the hate pours across his windshield? He sits in silence a moment considering the question.

"Nothing," he finally says. "A guy's got to make a living." He figures to stay in Ajo until it "gets hot."

You mean the high summer temperatures?

"No," he says.

Tom Childs, Jr., would live at Quitobaquito, a small spring on the border, or at Bates' Well near the tip of the Growler Mountains. He moved around a lot. He'd take a wife up to Gila Bend where the right kind of clay could be found. She'd get a few sacksful and they'd go home where she would fashion pots.

He kept coming back to Ajo as his home base.

The town sputtered along with maybe fifty people, mainly Indians and Mexicans. By 1911, only four American citizens lived there. Then a new leaching process meant Ajo ores were commercially feasible. The town had no real water and no one in town had any money. Tom Childs, Jr., had the key mineral claims.

But he lacked the capital to exploit the ore body and so he sold his mining claims to Phelps Dodge. Ajo entered a new kind of life.

The car glides down street after street and he ticks off the original names of the little subdivisions. A tumble-down house leans on a corner lot, the wood walls like a frail skin and the roof sagging. That, he explains, was originally a tent house, a plain-framed structure with canvas sides.

The green paint peels off the gray boards and the place has the look of a ghost that should be banished to a deep grave. Once everything in Ajo was simply tents, tent stores, tent houses, tent churches, tent tents.

The man keeps talking, sputtering out whiskey words and I sense the message in the stream of language because I have heard it again and again. In the West, nothing done by Americans is for keeps, everything—farms, cities, towns, mines, everything—constitutes a brief raid on the dry land and then becomes tumbleweed, ghost towns, lost mines, real estate empires that go up in flim-flam, and the like.

No one wishes to face this fact so they continually search the past for permanence, for memories to anchor their role in a terrain that does not care about them and has never needed them. They get half tanked, drive down a bleak street in a dying town and start talking tents.

Phelps Dodge owns most of Ajo and when the pit was roaring rented out 500 houses to the help. The rent was cheap. North of the company holdings is a patch where miners bought small pieces of desert and built their own homes. The town's few private businesses hug the highway on this stretch. But in the main, Ajo has relaxed in the security of Phelps Dodge's company stores offering easy credit, Phelps Dodge's hospital offering total medical care, Phelps Dodge's version of cradle to grave security. A woman of the town once told me her baby cost a buck and a half.

Now the strike has separated hundreds of the men from this security and the new hires taste lower wages. But the mind of Ajo, that bubble of consciousness appearing briefly over the beers in the saloons, clings to this habit of security. There is Ajo and there is this place the natives call "the outside world."

The man at the wheel ticks off the features of his town with pleasure. The town has seen many strikes and he figures it will weather this one. He is wrong but he is convinced he is right. The strike surfaces and then disappears and then surfaces again. Hundreds of people have left and hundreds come to Ajo. The Little League has lost half its players. Tires are slashed as the struggle grinds on. I go to interview a man and he answers the door with a gun in hand. The mine is marginal and, strike or no strike, will close in a few years. He admits these things but they do not register. He is an American, and therefore the future always looks good. He parks his car on a hill overlooking Ajo and the town glows like an ornament. Smoke flows listlessly from the big stack, the moon skimming across the white waves of pollution.

"I saw them build this road," he begins. "I saw that ground over there when there were no houses."

He rasps out an inventory of the streets and hills, of old Mexican Town, old Indian Town, old houses, old hotels, and old days.

"Change?" he roars. "Things always change. When I arrived decades ago, everybody lived in tents. World War II? Hell, there were gun emplacements all around the goddamned pit so we could make goddamn copper for the goddamn war. The pay? Hell, I made $11 a day, not an hour, a day.

"This town has always been a place where normal working guys could get on. Just today, I hired three cotton pickers from up along the Gila at Hyder, guys that had been making $3 an hour. And they're good men and they'll become part of this town. That's all this place has ever been about, people working, working hard."

He falls silent a moment as if challenging me to disagree with his words. He flicks a long ash off his cigarette and stares fiercely and protectively at the electric fires dotting Ajo below.

"I was proud," he suddenly erupts, "proud that this company was owned by just seven stockholders and we worked and made copper."

I let the boast pass and for the first time begin to feel a little warmth for the angry man. His roots are still deep in the colonial economy of the desert where everyone works for someone else, someone rich and eastern and as distant as the moon. The West of rugged independence has always been manned by hired hands who maintain their pride by hard work, insolence, and periodic bouts of violence. They own little or nothing but imagine they possess the endless landscape they see before them, and this succors them as they slave for profits that fatten clubmen along Wall Street. Phelps Dodge is still headed by a Yale man. The landscape, harsh, big, and seemingly limitless, continues to feed this illusion. In the West, every blue collar rides under a Stetson dream.

The Ajo man uses his glowing cigarette like a lecture pointer as he sketches the town's historical high points—that Ajo had segregated theaters until the 1950s, had segregated washrooms at the mine until the early sixties, had the men working twenty-six days straight and then two days off until the late seventies. Had some of the biggest drunken brawls in the desert to its credit.

The warm night hangs over the now quiet town.

"We were family," the man says.

John Greenway created the big copper mining operation in Ajo. A Yale man, he first worked for Carnegie Steel and rode with the

Rough Riders in Cuba. In 1910, he came to Bisbee, Arizona, as general manager of one of the copper mines. In 1917, he helped deport 1200 men on box cars when they struck. There was a war on, and the companies tarred them with the word traitor. They were dumped into the New Mexican desert and blacklisted.

He was a progressive Republican, one of the original Bull Moosers. By the 1920s, he was an active Democrat and a candidate for the vice-presidency in 1924. And he was Ajo. Soon the town had boomed to 5000 men in the mine.

Tom Childs took a different path. He prospected, ranched, and rambled. The sale of the claims made him prosperous and he fathered fourteen children by Sand Papago wives. Sometimes he would camp out on the desert surrounded by his Indian kin.

The rain dance meant a drum, fiddle, flute, and "a hideous sound." He witnessed an old man, wearing a mask made of a gourd, perform "with whoops and hollering." He saw another old man hop around like a toad and then suddenly grab a coal from the fire and pop it in his mouth—Childs could hear the sizzle of the hot chunk on his tongue.

Childs bought the grazing rights to 640 sections. He bought cars but never added oil to the crankcases. When they froze up, he walked away from them. The dead machines surrounded his ranch house like carcasses.

"Come on," he says. "Let's go to J.C.'s, Ajo's last remaining union bar."

For him this is a kind of boast—that he, the company man, will walk into a saloon of enraged strikers and he will be all right. He tells me this. He says, "You'll see."

The jukebox throws out country and the bar is lined with faces hardened by the strike. As he walks in, everyone looks him over. He has just parked his Lincoln Continental. The people at the bar have not cashed a paycheck in months and months.

Two guys get up and walk over to him. One guy is big, very big, and the strike is stenciled across his body like a gaudy tattoo. He stares from behind a three-day beard and then he embraces the man who boasts Ajo is family.

"And I want you to know," the big man says, "that I'm proud to be on the other side from you and if I wasn't my dad would be ashamed of me."

The company man orders up a round. He is smart enough to realize there are no clever words to use at this moment.

A Mexican guy makes the next move. I've interviewed him in the past—first during the long layoff, then in the early days of the strike, and finally at Christmas with a houseful of kids and no money for presents. His life, he has told me, is a shambles. But he is still firmly for the union. The Mexicans have a fierce devotion to the union. They remember those segregated changing rooms and being given all the low-paying jobs.

He gives an *embrazo* to the company man and then sweeps his hand toward the world outside the union bar and says, "I don't want to talk about that stuff out there."

The woman sitting next to the company man is strong union and she talks about her husband, a boiler-maker. He's up in Nevada at the moment with fifty or sixty Ajo men doing a repair job on an electric generating plant. They've offered him a permanent job but he wants Ajo.

She says he did twelve days work in a power plant in northern Arizona and made $3000.

"And you know," she continues, "he'd rather be in Ajo working a shift for Phelps Dodge."

The company man says little.

Out in the parking lot, the desert night blots out the barroom talk for a moment. The company man and the big union man lean against a truck and catch up on friendly gossip. But no one can keep it that tame.

"We, the union," the striker blurts out, "are right. We want an existence; we want pride; we want unity. We're down to the hard-core strikers. We're down to the guys who won't give in."

The company man and the union man kind of stand there, toeing the mark, and wait. They both seem surprised to meet and suddenly have the strike come between them. The warm glow of the beer is not enough to mask the future descending upon Ajo. The copper industry is dying. The union is dying. The whole way of life based on ripping up the earth for good wages and then going home to a com-

pany house after picking up a six-pack at a company store is all dying.
"Win, lose, or draw," the union man continues, "we won't give in."
But of course that hardly matters to anyone at all.

Tom Childs' kids grew and he hired a tutor, a college graduate out of Phoenix, to live at the ranch and teach them. As the children married, they built houses around the stone ranch headquarters and everyone ate at a communal table. Sometimes there would be forty or fifty people at a meal.

A Choctaw drifted through preaching the end of the world and the Second Coming of Christ. Childs listened hard to the message and then acted. He had a four- or five-room cement house built on a hill. He and the family gathered there and waited for the end. When the desert did not disappear under a raging sea, he grew impatient. Finally, he drove the preacher off and left the cement house to wait alone in the mountains for the final chapter.

He died in the 1960s stuffed with years, and at least fifty grand-children came to the funeral. The town hung a portrait of him.

Nobody quite knew what to make of the old man and his big family. He had essentially founded the place but he did not seem to connect to the smelter and mill and pit. The man who roamed with the Sand Papagos knew a country that had no common ground with company housing, free medical, and strong unions. He had seen the beginning of Ajo and then he took with him memories of the end of the desert people.

He left Ajo rooted in nothing but a big hole in the ground.

Now the desert is silent and the people have gathered in Ajo to make a buck, not to live out dreams, fantasies, and theories about salvation. The town sits on the edge of one of the nation's greatest wildernesses, thousands of square miles of desert to the west, but few locals ever venture into it. Like most Western towns and cities, Ajo is an oasis, a space colony that sits on the dry earth and reaches out with telephone, radio, and cable television to examine the world. It is not of the desert; it just happens to be in a desert.

The company man and I stumble into the town's Indian bar. He is determined to prove he knows his town.

The woman leans heavily against the bar and eyes a Budweiser longneck. She is a little stout but for a Papago, a people often cursed by obesity, quite trim. Her face is pleasant and smooth, the eyes almond, the skin a rich brown. A bunch of guys play pool at the far end of the bar and she points to one and says, "See him? He's a redneck."

She looks me over and asks, "Are you a white guy?"

The night has about run its course and she is pleasantly drunk. Just last week, she went to work for Phelps Dodge.

She rubs her fingers together and explains, "The money."

She has two kids. The welfare paid $283 a month and she could not make it on that. She knows the company man and they greet each other warmly.

Tonight has not been good for her. Earlier she stopped off at the Pizza Hut and her cousin's boyfriend tore into her for being a scab.

"I hate Ajo," she says softly, "but I was born and raised here."

She starts drawing a map of old Indian Town on a bar napkin. Once the place stood near the lip of the pit, a bunch of shacks going for $10 a month. Old timers claim that a rich Indian would rent two shacks and then throw up a ramada between them to create a Papago palace. Next to old Indian Town was old Mexican Town. And then fifteen or twenty years ago, the mine expanded and swallowed the district, and Ajo finally became integrated.

Ajo started with Indians. They would come here to get the copper ores for coloring their skin. But Ajo is going to end somewhere else.

She works slowly and carefully on her map.

She suddenly turns to me and announces, "I am an Indian."

She asks me if I want to go home with her.

The company man grabs my arm and says, "Let's go."

Tom Childs left a lot of family. He raised at least twenty-five orphans and sometimes his communal table had to feed seventy-five people. And after he died, his kin stayed in town and multiplied. In July 1972, a descendent, Philip Celaya, nineteen, was shot dead by the police. That same day the kid had gone out and bought a head-stone for his father's grave. The cops determined the killing was justifiable; the local Indians called it murder.

Dennis Banks, a leader of the American Indian Movement, came to Ajo to lead a protest. About two hundred Indians camped out at the Childs ranch. There were marches, protests, investigations, and when the paper work ended, the cops were officially cleared.

Over the years, Tom Childs' ranch had been chipped away by the government for a military gunnery range and other uses. Finally, only a fourth was left. The Bureau of Land Management ordered some of the buildings torn down. The whole Childs clan seemed eclipsed by the new Ajo and the new desert.

So it came as a kind of surprise to the town when they marched after Philip Celaya died. A hundred relatives showed up.

The company man is drunk now, very drunk, and I am falling down into a dark hole of booze. He still views me with contempt but it is a kind of friendly contempt. I am not of this town and I can never be of this town and he insists I recognize that fact. We stand in the parking lot outside the Indian bar and talk with a certain carefulness. He does not mention the Indian woman or the color line that briefly stood in my path and rang his alarms.

The desert has offered the American people many possibilities, not because they made something of the desert but because it offered a blankness, a clean sheet of map paper where they could live out their lives and not be bothered with other places or concerns. The fantasy of the inhabitants of the Old West and the New West is that they have built a culture rooted in the land. Of course, this was, and is, hardly ever true. Here people have largely lived isolated from the land in cities, mining camps, retirement communities, and irrigated agricultural districts. It would be difficult to find a region where more people worshipped the look of the landscape or hated and feared walking through the very landscape they admired. The desert is always the backdrop to the lives, but the lives are always lived in the pit.

And now this one particular life, Ajo, is becoming a corpse.

The company man seems finally at a loss for words. He has shown me his town and spoken his drunken piece.

He finally says, "This is a good town, a damned good town."

And then he hesitates and cocks an eye at me.

"Don't shit on me boy," he finishes and then he walks away.

Reasons to quit
The smoke and booze don't do me like before.

The band chases country music as the clock marches on midnight.
Couples nuzzle in the booths and drain longnecks and talk bubbles
through the blue air. Pool balls crack across the room as Saturday
night lurches toward the finality of closing time in the Tucson coun-
try-western bar.

The urban crowd is decked out in cowboy costumes, the boots that
never swung over a horse, the belt buckles sized off billboards. The
talk is by rote and words bounce back and forth about deep thirsts
and sexual fires.

The clientele are mainly construction workers and their ladies.
The woman next to me at the bar wears a black sequined dress and
she is different. Smooth skin shines on her back and in front, her
breasts spill out from a deep V-cut. Black net stockings hug her firm
legs and a slit on the skirt races up to her hip. The heels are high and
spiked.

Her face wears some years but looks good, very good. The hands
are small and faint blue veins stream over the tiny wrists to her
fingers.

She is a woman of some money and this fact is even more apparent
than her full breasts and firm legs. She tosses down her drink and the
ice cubes clink. The slender fingers reach out and rattle the car keys
on the counter. Outside, the parking lot is pick-ups except for her
white Corvette.

She tugs at her tight dress and her body squirms with pleasure
against the cloth.

Reasons to quit
The low is always lower than the high.

Every man in the bar wants her.

She sits on the stool facing the mirror and the beer signs and the men look up from their drinks with blank faces and hungry eyes. But no one makes a move. She is money. The clothes are money and the manner shouts money.

So they hold back. She drives that big Corvette parked outside and they drive trucks and favor faded Levis. She keeps rattling her keys and talking and the men offer little strings of words back at her. They want her so bad but they are afraid to move, afraid to be made fools.

She finally slides off her stool and staggers down the room, her hips swaying, and out the door. A few minutes later she is back wearing a blue sweat suit and blue sneakers. Her place at the bar is gone and she shoehorns into another opening. Bright chatter rolls from her lips and the men laugh but continue to keep back.

She gets up suddenly and sashays over to the pool tables. The shooters ignore her and pretend intense concentration on their shots. Her body looks perfect. She is a dream that has descended on them.

She turns abruptly, pulls her pants down to her knees, and moons the bar. No one makes a sound.

The music rumbles on, the night continues toward closing time. She sneers at the men, pulls her pants up, and goes out the door.

> And the reasons for quitting
> Don't outnumber all the reasons why.
>
> —Merle Haggard, "Reasons To Quit"

DESERTS

"If they move, kill them."

—William Holden as Pike Bishop
in *The Wild Bunch*

The thing happened this way. The man had been arguing with his brother in this country bar while his wife sat silent by his side. Then the man and his wife left and a cop walked over to the car the man and his wife had just entered.

The man pumped the bullets of a .44 magnum into the cop's chest and then the cop's partner killed the man. The woman sat there amid the glass fragments screaming but unhurt.

The story behind the shooting got kind of complicated—there was that argument between the brothers in the bar. I got into it as an afterthought. I'd been sitting on a porch with an editor and busily getting drunk on a Saturday night when I deduced there must be some reason for such killings. He smiled and said, "Why don't you find out?"

I spent the next day wandering around the country bar with a hangover and asking questions. The nearby homes were all old cars on blocks in the yards and sullen men with tattoos promising punch outs with their eyes. I smiled a lot and shuffled.

The answers came in grunts and nods and ran like this. The man who pulled the .44 magnum had allegedly been fucking his fourteen-year-old daughter and getting blow jobs from his nine-year-old son, or at least that was what the friends of the kids said. The father's brother had been having his share of the daughter too. The bartender in the saloon said she didn't really catch exactly what they were arguing over, just some family matter.

I kept walking down country roads and talking to everyone I met to get some background on the guy with the .44. The newspapers were hungry for a bit of color on the story since you had a citizen dead and a cop dead.

I talked to a neighbor. The guy was a former prizefighter and he lived on a couple of desert acres with nineteen pit bulls, each one of the dogs chained to his own stake and straining for a piece of my hide. The man was small and had the look of a mongoose.

We stood out there in the sun and the man called his daughter out from his trailer and had her tell me what she'd learned from the dead man's daughter, her best friend. She said the dead man with the .44 had been fucking the girl and then got real jealous when she found a boyfriend at the junior high. The girl wore a nice gingham dress and spoke with a voice as flat as a board.

I scribbled all this down.

I then asked the guy with nineteen pit bulls just what kind of fellow his dead neighbor had been, you know, a few details to flesh out a portrait.

He glared at me and said, "He was a prick."

I said, "Sure, but can you tell me what kind of a guy he was."

He snapped, "I just did."

Bone

THE NEWSROOM IS SUNDAY EMPTY and I pick up the phone and a voice tells me, "I've found that guy you're looking for and the bastard's resting down at the morgue right now."

The cop on the line crackles with the good cheer of a man who wants to believe there is a place for everything and now discovers everything is at last in its proper place. I am excited and disappointed, excited by the tidbit of news but sad because I cannot interview a corpse for good quotes and a little color.

"The lightning," the cop says, "that big electrical storm last Friday, well, you remember those people who got hit? Yep, he was one of them."

I call an editor, pass along this bit of information and sink back into the calm of Sunday afternoon. My packed bag sits next to the desk on the floor, my boots are polished, my slacks pressed, and I'm wearing my only good shirt, a pink number from Christian Dior. I'm ready to catch the afternoon flight out of Tucson to L.A.

Six days before a seven-year-old girl was riding her bicycle on a side street a block from her house when a car pulled up and then the girl was gone. Four days later a man was arrested in Texas on suspicion of kidnapping her. The fellow electrocuted by lightning in the park, well, he was said to have known the alleged kidnapper. And now I am flying to L.A. to check up on the alleged kidnapper's past—he was raised in California and his folks still live in L.A. The girl is still missing.

121

I spin in the office chair and look out the window, a slit near the ceiling that offers a patch of hot Arizona sky. There is no other link in this room to the earth, and the place is processed air mixed with the purrs, clicks, and pops coming off the computers. I love my job but I am growing ill from all the hours I have spent in this room. I feel very foolish about this matter, this sense of fatigue, burnout, illness. No one makes me do what I do. I like what I do. But I am losing my ability to do it.

I keep fleeing into the desert. The day before I rode my bicycle 100 miles and while climbing a mountain crank by crank, two javelinas, a piglike beast of the region, stormed out from the roadside and stood there hair bristling as they defended their territory. I drank their anger like a drug and the memory of that moment still stirs deep within me.

But after that ride and the animals standing in the road with their coarse hair against the brown landscape, I returned to my work, to using the phone as a weapon in my search for information. I returned to the missing seven-year-old, the man from California accused of whatever crime may have happened, to the hunt for the man I eventually discovered was slumbering in the city morgue. And I returned to these matters with pleasure.

All the signs are present now. I am drinking hard liquor and drinking a lot. I sleep very little, and sometimes fall asleep in a lawn chair out in the yard, whiskey in hand, somewhere around three or four in the morning. I awaken at 6 A.M. and go back to work. And I have this desire to weep, but I never do. I did not shed tears when I carried my father's body from the house. But now the desire is powerful and almost uncontrollable.

I mention these matters to no one.

When it started six days ago, I'd arrived at work at 6 A.M. hoping to finish a long piece on crimes against the elderly. I had a seventy-eight-year-old, partially blind woman who had been raped and good notes on how this event had altered her view of her neighborhood and of the human race in general. Her small house was full of collections—buttons, figurines, and the like—she would never see again, and her head was so full of dark memories of that one night that she could hardly speak. She told me she now never turned on lights at night in the hope no one would think she was home. I had thick

notebooks full of old men murdered for a few bucks, old men and
women mugged, old women raped. I knew I had good stuff.

That first day, an editor interrupted these reveries and sent me out
on a missing kid story, something about this seven-year-old grabbed
the afternoon before. I was to go to the police command center and
hook up with the search parties and file in time for first edition at
8:30 A.M. or surely have something for second edition. I drove over
there figuring the kid would be found in the first two or three hours
of light, a rag doll with a skinny body and thin arms lying crushed in
the sand of a wash, dress up over her head.

The thing took much longer and the days and nights melted into
each other. All the print and radio and television media sat around
the command center laughing and joking and trying to wheedle facts
from the cops. We were a kind of instant family, cops and media, all
keeping the same bad hours, eating the same stale doughnuts, drinking the same weak coffee. I spent a lot of time trying to run down tiny
leads, interviewing neighbors, trying to get to the family now safe
from the press behind a constant police-guard detail. Every day I
filed once or twice. Getting tidbits for the paper was like squeezing
water from a stone.

Psychics drifted into the command centers explaining vibrations
they'd felt and hungry for a piece of the publicity. Various possible
witnesses were buried by the police and I spent a lot of time ferreting
them out and hoping for a colorful detail. After two days, the family
called a news conference in their backyard, a small green plot with a
child's playhouse. The parents made a plea to whoever might be
watching television—please give our daughter back to us. The father
wore a stern mask; the mother clutched a big Cabbage Patch doll,
the kid's favorite. She began with little mother things about how nice
her daughter was and how she knew nobody would want to hurt her
and then she broke like a dish. She began to shake and nobody in the
media pack said a word. Then these sounds rattled out of her body,
deep, grinding sounds of pain. I have shot animals. Those kinds of
sounds.

When the day ended for me, it was usually long after midnight and
I would drink. Some of the reporters were women and a little sexual
electricity snapped and popped in the saloon air. But I felt dead to
such offerings. I had this vision in my head of the kid out there

somewhere under a mesquite, probably a mile or two or three from wherever I sat with my whiskey, the body sprawled, the flesh swelling up like a balloon, and perhaps by now, the maggots working the corpse. The flesh was a swirl of motion and energy as the little grubs converted the child back to earth.

I kept working and frittering away my time on feeble efforts to find a hook for a story, find a new slant for old grief. I bought a stuffed bear just like the one a witness claimed she'd seen the kidnapped child with and I rode around with that bear on the truck seat beside me. I would drive out in the desert and take walks thinking I might step on her. I was convinced I would have to step on her. The desert hides things well. When I was a boy I almost stepped on a dead steer before I noticed it. The body cavity rocked with maggots but for some reason I had not seen it or smelled it until I was upon it.

That's the way I saw the kid. The desert is just so proficient at swallowing everything—dead steers, ghost towns, small girls.

The drinking kept building and then the smoking came on. I had a 500-mile bicycle ride across the state to do in a week or so, but this looming ordeal could not stop my hunger for booze and cigarettes. I stopped eating and rode around in my truck with a portable computer so that I could write and file anywhere at any time. And I did.

I fell in love with this story. The day after they busted the suspect in Texas, the Tucson cops descended on a trailer where he had stayed while in town. The place was a dump and the two occupants came from central casting. The guy, gift-wrapped with tattoos and up on a couple of child-molesting charges himself ("a real scumbag," the cops offered brightly), said the suspect was weak on personal hygiene and he'd eventually booted him and his friend out because they stunk. The girl had eighteen years, big tits, and a t-shirt that announced I AM THE ONE YOUR MOTHER ALWAYS WARNED YOU ABOUT. She dabbled in prostitution. The couple said the suspect did a lot of coke ("Do I have to tell you that?" the girl whined). I filed from a nearby saloon. A few weeks later people from the neighborhood burned the trailer to the ground.

These were some of the scraps I took with me to L.A. I figured I'd dig up the suspect's past records since he had priors going back to his fourteenth year—mainly sex offenses. And I would try to locate his parents. We had no real address but the greater L.A. phone books offered some possibilities. The family promised real pay dirt since the dad was a retired general.

The plane had a flat tire before take-off, and we all got free champagne courtesy of the captain. Finally, the desert rolled under us like a spotted rug, a big beige expanse with clots of green where ironwood, mesquite, palo verde, and acacia had a toehold. I looked out over the city nestled in the land and knew within my gaze the child was rotting under some limb.

I drank airline miniatures but the stuff made no difference. My guts felt like hot stones and the booze just steamed off with little effect except the moral slap of a promised hangover. The plane flew westward over Papaguería, the reservation where 15,000 Indians explored alcoholism, suicide, homicide, and sixty percent unemployment in a playground the size of Connecticut. Then came Ajo, the Cabeza Prieta game refuge, and the military gunnery ranges. I looked down fondly at this mix of antelope, wild sheep, and cannon. To the south the El Camino del Diablo, the highway of the Devil, etched a faint trace against the land. This was an old immigrant trail where hundreds of people dreaming of California gold became mummies lining the route when their water proved not enough. For 150 miles the plane roared over ground empty of human beings, save wetbacks (in border Spanish *mojados*), sneaking north across the line with visions of stoop labor dancing in their hot heads. They don't always make it. A friend of mine has a photo of a nice skull grinning out on a creosote flat.

I wanted to jump out of the airplane and hit the ground. I wanted to roll in the dust, eat the dirt, stuff my mouth with sand, to lie there on the creosote flats in the 110-degree warmth and listen to the faint breezes work the slender wands of the greasewood. At night in this vision, my flesh would shiver as the temperature sank. The light would vanish from the sky and snakes would slither across the stones and nighthawks squeak by as they dined on insects. At first light, the coyotes would give the dawn song, always a frail thing in this part of the desert, and I would brew coffee and watch color bleed back into the land.

Mountains passed under the wing from time to time, sharp jagged

spines of stone, and then came the river and the smudge of green
hugging the Colorado River. Here I stopped looking; California conjured up no dreams for me.

Lights needled the L.A. Basin. Then came touchdown and a cab
ride out into the early evening. The taxi driver was Iranian and
worked the outer frontiers of the English language. At twenty-nine,
he'd been through four wives, and he pulled over from time to time
to phone and check on his current woman. We parked at a fancy bank
of condos by a marina where the bad man's parents might be found.
I'd had a hell of a time explaining to the cabby what I was trying to do
and finally blurted out "PERVERT, PERVERT" and made a circle with
thumb and finger and poked another digit through the hole. He
looked a little blank and I offered, "FUCK KIDS, FUCK KIDS," and he
slowly nodded his head knowingly.

None of the mailboxes in the lobby had the parents' name. I raced
my fingers over all the buzzers hoping someone would ring me up
through the locked door and in idle chatter give me a clue to their
whereabouts. No one answered my rings. I walked outside and suddenly the sea air filled my head with thoughts of lobster dinners and
plates of steaming mussels. I listened to laughter and good times
spilling off the docked yachts and caught glimpses of women in
bikinis enjoying the evening on deck. I strolled around the units and
finally found a woman having a drink on a second-floor balcony. She
told me no one with that name lived there.

We headed off into Brentwood where another possible address
was listed. Actually, I had several leads but the cabbie was convinced
about Brentwood.

The lawn flowed under a big arching tree and a curved walk led
past a glowing lamppost to the door of the quiet house. I grabbed the
brass knocker—the head of William Shakespeare—and waited for
someone to stir within. I did not know who lived here, just that he
had used the address briefly when he got out of prison.

A woman asked through the thick door, "What do you want?"

I said I was looking for anyone who knew this man. There was a
long pause and the door opened with the inch gap permitted by the
chain. She squinted out and I kept talking, talking, talking, diving
and shifting and seeking that one word, or phrase or sentence or
smile that would get me inside of that house. I pulled a picture of the

guy from my pocket, a police mugshot of a dour face buried in a beard with wild hair flying out in all directions.

I said, "Look, here is all I've got: a seven-year-old girl is missing and the man in this picture has been charged. I want to know more than this picture."

I heard a rattling of the chain, the door flew open, and this middle-aged woman stood glaring at me.

I asked, "Do you know this guy?"

She said, "I'm his mother."

She pulled me into a den, a room walled with bookcases and photos of a young boy with a smiling face and bright eyes. She snatched a picture from the shelf, a fourteen-year-old in a hockey uniform and shrieked, "He was a beautiful boy! A beautiful boy!"

I scribbled in my notebook and she kept speaking, oblivious of me and my pen, talking about how good he had been as a child, and then at fourteen he went off to military school and the drugs began, those drugs! and they ruined his mind and now this, now this thing—she hoped the girl was all right. God, she hoped the girl was all right.

"How do you think we feel?" she said.

Then it was over. She said you must leave, leave right now. His father will be back from walking the dog at any moment and his heart is not good. He cannot take this. He cannot take any more. Go! Go! And I was slowly ushered toward the door.

I did not want to leave. The house smelled right, the lawn made so many good promises, and the books in the dark wooden cases of the den gave the look of a safe, decent womb. This was the house I had always wanted to be raised in, the quiet place on the side street where culture floated in the air like some bacillus infecting everyone with its fine notions of the world.

I went out down the curved pathway and climbed into the cab already writing the story in my head and as the car wheeled down the street, an old man with a dog froze in the headlights. He stared at me like I was an enemy tank invading the security of his ancestral village. The eyes flashed through his glasses with a mixture of fear and hatred. He knew I had scaled the ramparts protecting his world.

I could not have felt better.

I filed around midnight and then hit the bricks on the Santa Monica harbor dreaming of a nightcap. The nearest bar was closed.

The whole harbor area seemed already in bed with sidewalks empty of everything but bums and bag ladies stretched out for the night. I pleaded through the door and the guy let me in. He poured me a water glass of scotch, on the house.

Sleep came around 2 A.M. and I got up at 5 A.M. and headed into downtown L.A., hungry for more material. There were shrink reports, court reports, prison reports, DA reports, cop bust sheets, photos at the scene, parole officer comments, a fourteen-year record of a man who from adolescence on could not seem to stay out of children's pants. The reports noted 200 acid trips, homosexual love affairs, and various doings. The accused speaking through the jargon of the reports figured sex was not too bad for kids since he himself had been seduced by a guy when he was fourteen. The old files held exquisite details of six-year-olds sprawled under bushes with panties down, of a seven-year-old boy who the guy allegedly sucked off and then insisted go down on him while he corkscrewed his thumb up the kid's ass. I felt like a miner who had hit a heart of gold. Afterward, one of the DAS took me out for a drink. We entered a Greek joint where all the men wore three-piece suits and all the women were much younger, well-dressed, and had the hard eyes of the hunt for Mr. Right.

"Hey," my companion shouted at the bartender. "This guy's from Arizona and it seems we shipped one of our perverts to his town."

"Hey," hooted the bartender. "Way to go!"

And he slammed down my drink, on the house.

The afternoon flight back to Tucson aroused once again my dreams of the desert. I stared down at the sterile ground and saw the possibility of lust returning to my life.

I have a simple definition of health. I see a rare steak, a bottle of red wine, and a woman and I smile at all three. The night air will be rich with scent and every gesture will be laden with potential adventure. Somewhere in the desert a table is set and a slight breeze sags with the perfume of flowers. Insects strike up a steady whirring but the sound is muted and discreet like chamber music. There is a tablecloth but we never spill our drinks. We get drunk but do not talk loudly. The moon washes everything with pale light and my shoes settle into the soft earth. We are in a slight clearing ringed by ironwood and palo verde. A game trail nicks the corner of our space and my fingers explore the delicate lines of the crystal ware. I look up and see a coyote padding down the path. He glances over but does not pause. And then he is gone. The wine slides down my throat rich with fruit and sunny days. We say nothing memorable. The steak tastes of mesquite. There is that tablecloth—I cannot tell the color —and we never spill a drop on the clean surface. I am certain of this last fact.

Months later, they found the girl's body under a mesquite tree, at least some of it, a hunk of skull, some ribs, and the jaws. Thank God for the jaws with those little teeth that neatly matched the dental charts.

By then, I was long gone to where I always go, the desert. I haven't got much theory on why I go to hot, dry, empty places.

Just a lot of miles.

The Tucson motel lingers by an old highway. The nearby Interstate has taken the travelers away and now the place caters to lovers looking for a nooner and three-hour affairs paced by in-room pornographic movies.

At first the fat woman hesitates about showing me the room but she gives way. She apologizes for the smell of bleach; she has worked hard to get the blood off the cement-block walls. The water bed is stripped of sheets and the big blue bladder dominates the room. The floor is tile. The television hangs from the wall beaming "Deep Throat" and "Tropic of Passion."

In the bathroom, there is still a puddle of blood on the floor—she will get to it in time. I look in the refrigerator and discover a frozen bottle of Budweiser in the freezer as if someone has slipped in a brew for a quick cool and then forgotten about it.

A man and woman lived here with the woman's twenty-one-month-old boy. They were maintaining the domestic drives of our culture in the inhospitable soil of the Sunbelt where half the marriages end in divorce and constant movement is the meaning of life. Two days ago, she went to her shift at a strip joint and he got tired of the kid somehow. He bashed the boy against the walls until the child died.

The woman says she has done a lot of work on the room, just that puddle in the bathroom left to clean up. She and some friends have gone to a discount store and gotten some little clothes for the child's burial. The mother and boyfriend are in jail. They fled but did not get far.

We walk back to the motel office. She shows the clothes. I tell her they look real nice. A guy comes in, sunglasses, tie, shiny suit. Outside I see a forty-year-old woman in heels, her body curved but sagging. She appears ill at ease. The guy says, "We don't want the room with the little boy."

At the funeral the casket is open. The kid looks real pale and has a teddy bear. His natural father has come down from Phoenix. He wears a black shirt, white tie and says the mother just took off with the kid, just like that. He says he first met her in Denver and they lived together and then the kid came. They went on to Phoenix. And she ran off.

I ask him where the woman was raised.

He says he never asked.

The mother finally arrives and is escorted by the cops to an ante-chamber where she can see the casket but not be seen. She has red hair, a thin, small body, and looks to be about twenty years old.

After the service, they whisk her out the back. Her hands are cuffed and she shrieks and shrieks and shrieks.

Black

Other people will do the thing that we must not do,
  Namely kill the earth.
And you will not be the ones to kill the staying earth.
I will leave it to them.
And they will do it.
And these will kill the staying earth.
And even if you don't know anything
And you just be feeling fine
And you will see it when it happens.

—The words of Elder Brother (I'itoi),
according to a Piman shaman
who repeated the prophecy to whites
on the Gila River in the 1920s.

THE THREE STONE MONUMENTS can wait. I crawl under the limbs of the small ironwood tree and celebrate the shade. The air still tastes of the Gulf of California, seventeen miles away across the dunes. My fingers rip open a packet of M&M's and I devour them and the sweet mash quickly floods my tired body with energy.

We are in the malpais, a lava chaos reaching up toward Sierra Blanca Pass. The small tree promises the first real shelter in a day.

133

The black rock rakes our boots and throws the heat back into our faces. A cold front spares us normal weather, and the April sun pours down with a gentle 85 degrees. Once a weather station in Sierra Blanca Pass stalled at 134 degrees.

We intend to walk 130 miles from Puerto Peñasco on the Gulf in Sonora, Mexico, to Ajo, Arizona, the copper town busy dying from bad markets and bad strikes. We are following a trail laid down before the birth of Christ and used until around 1450 A.D. by a people called the Hohokam. The Hohokam are all gone now, fallen into rumor, scattered ruins, and museum cases. They left us without a clue and the mystery of their passing sometimes bites into our peace and brings on the bad night thoughts.

The monuments are another matter: slabs several inches thick tilt against each other like drunken remnants of a Stonehenge. They stand two or three feet high on the black rock under the hot sun. We have seen nothing like them before, and there is no record of their existence among the writings of the archaeologists who have wandered into this country. No one will probably ever explain them and they will wait in this place century after century to taunt the occasional drifter coming through.

They are part of the ribbon of energy that is the shell trail, a strand worn by human footprints from the waters of Adair Bay on the Gulf to the rivers of central Arizona, the Gila, the Salt, the Verde.

This ancient shell business has brought us to this place. The facts are few and simple. Once human beings walked down into this country and gathered shells at specific sites in Adair Bay and then walked home. They made the shells into ornaments, amulets, various objects of beauty and power.

In our twentieth-century eyes this smacks of business but for them it was probably best understood as a quest. The people passed this way seeking visions and dreams and the shells became a door opening up the secret regions of their heads. Southwestern cultures once had many such journeys—salt journeys, eagle killings, shell journeys—all ventures leading to places off the map but deep in the country of the heart. This is a game almost no one plays anymore. But then the world that risked such journeys has been temporarily obliterated.

The old ones crossed a country with almost no living water, a country of thousands of square miles with one tiny spring, no flowing rivers, no creeks, brooks, bogs, or small ponds. A desert of three to nine inches of rain a year.

The people who performed these feats came, as we do, from the moister areas of southern and central Arizona. There they, like us, gathered and lived in large communities, raised crops by massive irrigation systems, threw up a world, and found a way to speak to their gods.

We follow their trail but not their way. Our backpacks are made of nylon, our water bottles ward off punctures with an exotic plastic, and our food is freeze-dried packets.

We are industrial men resting one April day in the final years of the twentieth century under a tiny ironwood tree by a trail thousands of years old. We have come from a desert city of more than half a million where human beings gather and thrive around deep holes punched into the earth and busily drain ancient aquifers. We come from a city where each and every human being requires around one hundred and fifty gallons a day. For five days, we will live on one or two gallons a day.

I look over at the monuments. They are a message sent that I will never receive.

I know no desert language. I am the interloper, the refugee, the tourist, the present that denies the past.

I speak a tongue forged on another continent, one rich with words spawned in green forests under gray, soggy skies. I do not belong here. I just have these longings.

The trail becomes a riddle as we enter an eight-mile lava chaos. To the west stand the peaks of the Pinacate, a 650-square-mile volcanic wilderness where no man has lived since a last Sand Papago hermit fled in 1912. To the east, the lava tongue ends in the creosote flats of the valley. We speculate whether the Indians crossed the jagged hummocks of lava slashed with wide crevasses and tortured footing or took the long way out into the valley and back around the black rock.

But we can feel the answer.

They took the easy way, not the short way, the easy way, the route that saved the energy in their bodies and the water in their small clay canteens. We sense they lived a life and walked a logic that dominated most human beings until well after the Renaissance, the logic of people who had nothing to fall back on beyond that which was immediately available. We are as arrogant as their gods and can live differently.

I've been to this country before. Years ago, I wrote a book called *Killing the Hidden Waters*, a volume that talked about water and the ways different cultures used water. The book started in a research institute amid heaps of reports, elegant graphs, and piles of computer printout. The statistics that marched across my desk always presented ways to avoid the world of muscle, sweat, and thirst. I was dazzled by the sheer weight of the numbers, but I did not believe them.

I went walking—walking mountains, walking bajadas, walking deserts, walking with scientists, walking with Indians and most often walking alone. I learned with my feet what the books, reports, symposiums, commission conclusions, and studies skirted: that resources are limited and that technology, invention, and industrial voodoo cannot increase the amount of a resource but simply accelerate the destruction of a resource through consumption. The well does not make water; it mines water.

The book wandered through the culture of the Papago, the Comanche, and the Europeans who entered the Southwest. Resource problems were explained as the products of cultures, not the creation of the land itself. The desert, which produced a society for the Papago based on abundance, based on enormous sharing between people, was the same desert that became a wasteland terrifying early white settlers with fears of water shortages.

Once the new people, my people, plugged into the shortages of water buried in the earth or fuels buried in the earth or metals buried in the earth, all these worlds exploded and the old ways and old customs and old fears became historical footnotes and historical junk.

We called this explosion progress.

I had dreams that the book would function as a primer that would teach people that they did not have a water problem or a resource problem but a water reality, a resource reality. And then it was published and disappeared into a few libraries and a handful of book reviews and I stopped thinking about water and water reports. I stopped thinking about such matters because I realized I had made a mistake. The Southwest that was furiously destroying its water table and gutting its soil and looting its minerals did not falter when faced with these facts. It trembled with the energy of rapid growth. The cities based on dwindling water supplies filled with more and more people. The wolf I imagined standing at the door seemed to become a mirage.

I learned something.

The industrial culture that made me and controlled my mind possessed a mentality of such power that it was immune to simple warnings, simple messages of future problems and inevitable ruin. As the water tables continued to sink across the region, as the rivers were taxed beyond their flows, people did not back off with their thirsts. They did not even become alarmed.

They said something would turn up.

They said something always had.

I watched them and took notes and discovered my idea of the world was far too simple. I learned that under the skin of my computerized, high-technology society lived a soul and the soul feasted on a world of its own, a world of dreams. I visited the murders in the motel rooms, the ranchers killing the mountain lions, the farmers raping the soil and poisoning the land, the politicians balancing the budgets against their ambitions, the real-estate czars drawing new cities on empty plats like lords, the rush and tumble of human hunger in this new word, Sunbelt, and I realized that none of these people believed in the desert or lived in the desert or heard the rasping whispers of the landscape stretching just beyond their safe city streets or neat furrows.

And they were truly my people, and I shared at a level beyond conscious thought or personal decision their visions and their hungers. But I kept going back into the desert.

And the desert teaches other dreams.

We decide to cross the lava chaos, take the short route and the eight-mile hike eats up hours. The footing is bad, the crevasses become so many small canyons with descents and ascents that the skin is scraped and the flesh bleeds. We do not see a single human artifact on this stretch. We are the first ones foolish enough to think a straight line is the shortest distance between two points. Instantly upon leaving the rock jumble, the Indian trail comes in from the east, swinging toward the black mountain from the smooth valley below. We have learned a lesson any child once knew.

The trail lances toward Tinaja Cuervo, Raven Tank, a few holes in

the rock that trap the phantom rains and then hold the moisture for
weeks and months at a time. These slimy pools are the water in this
country and for thousands of years feet have pounded toward them
for relief.

We walk into the sunset hungering for Tinaja Cuervo.

A nighthawk moans on the rock nearby. I lie in my bag near
campfires 10,000 years cold. Sleeping circles, stone barriers raised
against the evening winds, dot the landscape. Bits of pottery lie
scattered and a short way off is a pile of cremated sheep bones, one
more mystery. This desert offers the only place in the Western
Hemisphere where ancient hunters cremated their kills. No one
really knows why. I finger the vertebrae off a long-dead desert
bighorn. The bone is rough, the surface blackened by the fire.

I lean over and adjust my stove. The burner hisses with bottled
butane from Colorado. I pour boiling water into an aluminum pouch
holding a freeze-dried dinner from Oregon.

Above my head, the nighthawk skitters after insects and behind
me coyotes bark in the hills. The stars sizzle in the sky and satellites
course across the heavens on their errands.

I rest by ancient campsites in my nylon cocoon stuffed with goose
down. Energy systems twirl around me: hawks chasing moths,
flames feeding off fossil fuels, food produced in fields I have never
seen, space machines slipping toward the horizon. I am in the place
of the ancestors but the knowledge in my head walls me off from the
world that surrounds me. I can visit this place but I will never know
it and eat it and worship it. My energy systems cast a larger and more
distant net.

To the north, one hundred miles or so, the Gila River sputters
across Arizona, a stream totally consumed by irrigated agriculture,
one whose course is often marked by a dry, sandy bed. To the west
and north, the Colorado River storms down from the mountains
swollen by melting snows and is siphoned off by dams and canals and
aqueducts for the thirsts of Los Angeles and the fields of the Imperial
Valley and electric needs of the Southwest. To the northwest lies the
Colorado delta, a place described by Aldo Leopold in the 1920s as the
great wilderness of the Southwest and today a scene of death, a
raked-over region which the consumed river does not penetrate for
decades at a time. Cutting across Arizona is the Central Arizona
Project, a $3.6 billion canal which will deliver water from the Colo-

rado to the central portions of the state where God neglected to put the river in the first place.

Far to the northeast, I can see the glow against sky caused by Phoenix, a blob parading as a city. The carpet of subdivisions and malls and factories sprawls across the bones of an abandoned Hohokam community. And just to the east, I see nothing but I know what is there: the *ejidos*, the collective communities founded on the edge of this volcanic desert by the Mexican government so that landless peasants from the interior can finally pretend to have some land. At first these *ejidos* were going to be irrigated farms but the deep wells sucked up the skimpy aquifers in a few years and salt water from the sea began to rush into the new underground void. Now they are toying with cattle and goats, and soon these beasts will eat the desert into the ground. Already, the peasants have ranged over the Pinacate and cut down the forests of ironwood killed by a drought decades long. Now their new animals will devour the few plants with a toehold in the malpais.

Everywhere I look this night I hear the distant thunder of the twentieth century's rush into the desert, the last pocket of space left in the idea of the frontier.

To object to this act is to cut one's own throat. No one will listen to such a voice. The logic of my time is industrialism and everything will be turned to account, even the hard ground of the Pinacate and the Sonoran Desert that carpets this slab of the Southwest with thorns, sand, and the dreams of people long dead and gone.

I fall back into my sleeping bag and let my eyes drift across the heavens.

Eight satellites steal through the sky in three minutes.

The white people were the very last to speak. It was said that, like a younger child, they were cry babies. So the creator did everything to soothe them. Hence, they are richer than any of the Indians.

—Creation tale of the Maricopas, a tribe of the middle Gila.

Coyotes bark at dawn and a nighthawk lands thirty yards from my bed. The morning light reveals the ancient trails crisscrossing the flat toward Tinaja Cuervo. Sleeping circles dot the ground and here and there shells gleam where some human hand pitched them aside centuries ago. We are clearly on the route and take enormous satisfaction from this simple fact.

Doves streak across the orange sky heading in for water. We load up and trudge down to a slender canyon looking for Cuervo.

It is an easy thing to miss. A giant ironwood hovers over the rock pool and the green water is a dab twelve feet by six. Stone walls seventy-five feet high hem in this dream of moisture. At my feet is a pottery fragment and I peer down and listen to the roar of bees, the whirr of hummingbirds as life celebrates the stuff of life. I glance at my boots and see a shell fragment. Nearby lies a broken metate where the women once ground seeds. This casual trash left by other wanderers bewitches me and I feel them very near and yet very far away. We take nothing—not because of strictures by archaeologists to protect a site and not because of laziness. We have this dumb hope that if everything is left intact others might some day stumble in and feel the same sensations.

Across the canyon, a hole in the rock displays a crude nest of twigs. Suddenly an owl flaps out into the growing light and flies blindly into the sun.

It is not easy to comprehend the power of this speck of stagnant water. For millennia, such green, scummy dabs of fluid were the line between life and death. It is like picking up a bow and arrow and thinking, "This is a good weapon," and putting from one's mind rifles, cannons, and bombs.

I swallow half a liter from my plastic canteen.

The land is slowly becoming magic. The first day of the trek, I wallowed in depression. I remembered warm beds and electric lights and flowing taps and found the dunes a forbidding country. Now this mood is gone and I accept the rock and hot desert as an adequate world. I stop thinking of cold beers and thick steaks. The slimy water begins to look very, very good.

Water is the big ticket item out here. To the north on the edge of the Lechuguilla Desert, men drank at Tule tanks for thousands of years. Then came the Americans streaming westward toward the gold and possibilities of the California coast and in the 1860s, a Mexican dug a well at the tanks and began selling the water. A year or two later, another man came out of the searing creosote flats and cactus-covered slopes with a huge thirst.

He shot the Mexican dead.

Today, Tule tanks is a way station for illegal immigrants walking north forty to sixty miles toward jobs in the fields or back rooms. The march toward dreams of wealth has shifted direction but not intention. About two years ago, I was there and found a water bottle, much like my own, stashed in a shelter by the well. The container looked like something left for the next traveler who might be in need of a drink.

I poured the fluid out on a rock and the rock sizzled from the splash of hydrochloric acid.

We leave Cuervo soon after dawn and follow an old trail that heads down into the flats and arcs toward Tinaja Romero. The rotten antler of a deer lies by the path. The land that seems so empty, not only of life but of any possibility of life, slowly forces the eye to notice. In the dunes the day before, we stumbled across the skeleton of a coyote asleep on the sands. Snakes darted through the bramble and a tightly coiled sidewinder looked up from beside my foot. Thorns tore at our legs and soon they were covered with the red smear of blood. Suddenly, we came upon an Indian campsite—hearth, shells, broken pots, all spread over the ground like refuse from a picnic the previous weekend rather than from previous centuries.

Today is more of the same as our feet lead us into a past that is immediately present. At Romero tank, the water is almost gone, a scant green puddle. On the nearby rocks, Hohokam pecked outlines of shells into the stone a thousand years ago. We stop and eat our lunch of candy bars and salami while yellow warblers dart through the gray leaves of the ironwood.

A raven croaks and then his shadow passes over my reclining body.

Just past Romero, a golden wheat field sweeps along the wash between two black tongues of the lava flow. No irrigation produces this crop. No well gushes forth the buried hydrologic treasure of the earth. This is something the Papagos called *ak chin*, floodwater farming where human beings cast down seeds after the rain and hope the plants grow and flourish before the desert winds dry out the soil. For centuries and centuries this was the nature of farming in much of the Southwest. Now such practices have been vanquished and made foolish by the agribusiness dreams that drain the American and Mexican ground of the region. The field is a living fossil, a garden planted in the manner of people long gone from most of the land.

Two days ago, I met the farmers in Puerto Peñasco. The Romeros live in a cool house on the shifting sands near Adair Bay. Stalls lining the road advertise shells for sale and tout "FIREWOORCKS" to visiting American tourists. Since 1946, the Romeros have worked this field and before them Indians probably puttered here for centuries. But this is still desert and for seven years in the seventies drought brought crop failure. Now the rains have returned in their erratic way and the field blazes with wheat.

At the Romeros' home, children and adults clustered around us in the living room and offered us their hospitality. The old woman who heads the clan sat on the sofa shifting her cane from hand to hand as she spoke. In the next room, a television roared.

They were a link with a lost world but they did not understand this fact. Scientists from the University of Arizona monitor their field to discover the simple truths countless tribes of the Southwest once knew. The Romeros were producing food off the annual offering of the land instead of off the underground storages created by thousands of years of rain.

This makes them freaks.

We walk across the wheat and return to the creosote. Soon our march swings back into the malpais and then without warning comes Suvuuk, the next tank on the ancient trail.

Suvuuk is dry.

We crawl under the ironwood trees, eat salami, drink cocoa, wait out the heat of the day. The front is still holding and the temperature does not budge past 90. I am traveling with Bill Broyles, a high school English teacher in Tucson and a student of this dry country. He has tasted some of the pleasures and some of the pains.

Once when the summer heat hit 120 degrees, he took cover under a mesquite tree at midday. After a while he noticed a jackrabbit sharing his shade only a few feet away. Eventually the jack became spooked by the closeness of a man and tore off under the blazing sun for about twenty yards. Then the animal stopped, reconsidered, and hopped back to the shade. He and Broyles sat there together for hours until the late afternoon eased the force of the sun.

Once Broyles came out of the Lechuguilla to a buried cache of water stored in plastic bottles. A coyote had dug up this reserve and ripped the jugs to shreds. Broyles almost died on his walk out.

All this is easy to forget in the shade at Suvuuk as the stove hisses under a cup of cocoa and a Costa's hummingbird hovers a foot from my red t-shirt. I have no simple handle on the desert. Murder, rape, robbery, capital punishment, high interest, the stock market—all these matters produce quick and easy opinions. But not the hot, dry ground. I have walked hundreds and hundreds and hundreds of miles in the desert and yet my thoughts about it are very few and I spend very little time thinking these thoughts. At noon when the sun is cooking and the light a glare, I do not like the place. Toward evening it grows more pleasant. The vegetation tears my flesh and usually seems monotonous. Wildlife is generally not abundant and large mammals are seldom glimpsed in the drier stretches. And the water is almost always silent. It just lays there in scummy pools or is not there at all. The desert fires my appetite for life and here I know this fact: the desert is where I want to die, where I do not fear death, do not even consider it. Here death is like breathing. Here death simply is.

After an hour or two, we push on and leave the malpais. The Hohokam trail bends east to the dry bed of the Rio Sonoyta where at certain sites digging in the sand can produce a miserable kind of water. The Indians go that way but we move straight ahead across a huge creosote flat.

The wind is at our backs and in the afternoon hours this is what I see: four jackrabbits. The rodent holes are all collapsed, the animals driven back for the moment by drought.

At dusk we pitch camp on the flat, a matter of dropping our backpacks, spreading out our sleeping bags, and firing up the small stove. The moon rises and a breeze plays gently with the limber branches of the greasewood under a light like thin milk. This is among the very best of times.

These barbarians lived in their paganism without any beliefs, without shelter, without authority, without knowledge of origins, without village nor houses, in the mountains and the open country…each obeying the impulses of his degeneracy and his sensual nature.

—Padre Lambert Hostell, Mission San Luis Gonzaga, Baja California, 1737, commenting on the Pericu, a people some anthropologists liken to the original inhabitants of the Pinacate.

We have finally walked away from our lives. The jobs that chain us to desks and telephones fade from our conversation and we study more immediate matters. My feet are butchered from the fifty-pound backpack and the twenty- to thirty-mile days. My belly never gets enough food.

And I cannot stop walking. I want to keep moving into the country although all I seem to do is move through it. I fall each night into a dreamless sleep and wake each day in a dream. The landscape comes from the far side of the mind—black slopes, blue sky, burning sun.

We stumble through messages: the stone monuments at Sierra Blanca Pass, the petroglyphs at Tinaja Romero and near Suvuuk a 350-foot man with an enormous sexual organ lies sketched against the earth by an outline of stones. This is a fantasy world for me, some wild part of myself and my blood that I sense was walled off by stout doors and barriers during the early days of the Industrial Revolution when my people were lured from the village festivals and dark rites into the mills. I lie under the stars and I can almost hear a heavy steel door clang in some factory and the desert freedom disappears from view.

The past, the wilderness, the sting of thirst, the grip of hunger have become an exotic in my world and in my life. I think back to Secretary James Watt at Glen Canyon Dam so easily celebrating the big cement block choking the river. And Dave Foreman of Earth First! trying by language to conjure up a world that has dropped below our horizons.

"We have the vision." I hear Foreman roaring. "We have the daring....We will see Glen Canyon alive and free, flowing and green in our lifetimes because we can do what we will to do.

"The other thing is we've got the ethic, we've got the courage...to put our bodies between what we love and the agents of destruction."

No we don't.

We are beginning to realize what we have lost with our wonderful inventions and our monstrous new powers. We are becoming more and more aware that our civilization destroys the foundations that support it by devouring the earth and the things of the earth.

But we don't have the courage to back away, to stop, to restrain ourselves. I know I don't.

It is just that finally I know, I truly know, that my world cannot last and this dry, hard ground around my camp can and will. So I visit the past to taste the deeper present and prospect the inevitable future.

I stretch out on the creosote flat north of Suvuuk where the giant stone man waves his cock at the gods and I hear Foreman talking in my head. I fall asleep by Stone Age highways.

At dawn, the temperature has fallen to 54 degrees but the day comes on strong. We march across the flats toward the dry river. Five days before, Bill cached food by a shallow pool in the river, a puddle swarming with fish. Now we arrive and find the river a pad of dry, cracked mud and big bird tracks explaining where the fish have gone.

Time and motion take over completely now. All the details on the map begin to blur. We pass through low hills and then comes the two-lane highway following the line and then the barbed wire fence separating nations. We move up a bajada, scramble a boulder-choked drainage and come to Agua Dulce Spring, the last gasp of living water for anyone traveling the hundred miles westward to the Colorado River. The spring is maybe a yard square and defiantly hosts cattails within a few feet of a big saguaro. The bones of a mule deer lie just below.

We sleep in a nearby pass and then drop into the Growler Valley. The walking now comes in twenty-five- to thirty-mile chunks. The days start at dawn and end at twilight when we throw down our bags wherever the darkness finds us. Sleep becomes a drug. Shells dot our line of advance and the horizon seems unreachable. The Growler Valley presents a thirty-three-mile-long slog through creosote. We walk past the antler of a mule deer, the horn of a desert sheep, and the hearths and sleeping circles of men lost to time.

In three days, we see only two human footprints that are not our own. No aircraft crosses the sky. No engines purr. The valley floor is all but dead. The rains this spring have been slight and in thirty-three miles I find only two living specimens of buckwheat, normally a common annual. The sun heats up and the temperature pushes past 100.

We do not care. It is three in the afternoon and I lean against a mesquite near an Indian camp—the old fire-blackened stones a few

yards away, broken shells scattered everywhere—and try John
Reed's *Insurgent Mexico*, a 1914 account of his time with Pancho
Villa's rebels. Reed, the Harvard man hungry for revolution, writes:

> And there was a sullen, Indian-faced woman, riding sidesad-
> dle, who wore two cartridge belts. She rode with the *hombres*—
> slept with them in the cuartels.
> "Why are you fighting?" I asked her.
> She jerked her head toward the fierce figure of Juan Reyes.
> "Because he is," she answered. "He who stands under a good
> tree is sheltered by a good shade."

I look out at a vacant patch of desert pavement, a big circle of small
stones that have choked off all possibility of plant life. The stones are
coated with a thin varnish and gleam. I recline in the shade of my
good tree and read of men and women dying seventy years ago for
ideas or at least for shade.

"It is almost impossible to get objective about the desert," Reed
warns.

We keep walking, walking, walking and our rest stops become
fewer and we take no breaks in the oven heat of the afternoon. We
are possessed by the country, or at least it comforts us to think so.

But of course, we are tourists, and soon we will return to the city,
to faucets that never fail, to thermostats that automatically control
air temperature, to machines that move our bodies, to stores that
peddle food.

All across the Southwest human beings now live in these oases that
draw little from their immediate surroundings save the weather. The
landscapes Bill and I have traversed have no messages or values that
interest such communities. They are a kind of bad memory left
behind a century ago, a nightmare world where people once lived off
the land and thus had to live with the land. These memories have
been exiled from our consciousness.

But one thing is clear to me as I sleep in the Growler Valley amid a
sea of brown, parched plants. One day, this exiled world will return.
When the aquifers have been milked, when the coal and oil beds
have been drained, when the rivers collapse from the repeated muti-

lations, when the fields fall into soil exhaustion, when the boom ends not with a bang but a desert wind, then they will be waiting.

They can wait a long, long time.

This is their place.

> *Yonder far I ran.*
> *Walked and ran.*
> *Iron stretched out.*
> *Then I beside it ran.*
> *Nowhere did it end.*
> *It stretched out.*
>
> —Papago song about rails when the trains first
> came into the country.

It ends after five days when we walk out into the small town of Ajo. These things always finish the same way and leave me with the same thought: why is the desert such a tiny compartment in my life? On a map the straight line stretches 110 miles but on the ground we have walked 130 miles or more. We are very tired now.

Easter Sunday slumbers over Ajo as the darkness thickens. We come out of the desert around 10 P.M. and the sounds of the small town bash our innocent ears. The hum of the refrigerator in a saloon thunders, the blaze of electric lights blinds us, and the barking of the dogs seems never ending. And people are everywhere, their homes, voices, cars, smells, marks. We are crushed by the sheer numbers of people.

For days we have joked about tables, menus, and cold beer. Now the dream roars in our ears and we do not want it.

We empty our canteens and walk into a restaurant and bar. I throw down three beers very fast and order fried shrimp. The desert slips away.

A man sits down and announces he is from Oregon. He smokes Camels and his face is lined and the nose red. He says he did sixteen years in the Army and now he is out and free and heading for Florida, just kind of bumming around in his old station wagon. He wants to know about the desert.

Where can he camp? Where can he park and not be rousted by cops or bothered by anyone? Cutting across Nevada he pulled over for a nap and suddenly these guys in uniform were hassling him and telling him he had to move on, something about a nuclear test site he thinks.

"Can't a man find a place to sleep in his own country?" he snorts.

And then he drops this subject and is off busily talking about his trip. He has $2000 and thinks maybe Florida. Then he'll hit some spots he used to know in Chicago, some great taverns. Who knows?

He plans to be on the road two months, just bumming around.

What the hell, the country is a piece of cake.

After the country was settled and the feasts instituted, I'itoi returned underground. He has occasionally appeared since then, when his help was needed. Once, after the railroad came through Papagueria, he was seen, in the guise of a little old man, driving away the game to safety.

—Ruth Underhill, *Papago Indian Religion*

From his office he sees the capitol's copper dome and the march of Phoenix outward under a canopy of smog. The hair is silver, the body solid and trim, a cargo carried easily despite sixty some years. The smile is perfect, disarmingly perfect. Keith Turley is the boss at Arizona Public Service Company. He gives electric power to almost half the citizens of the state. His desk is large, fine wood, and clean. He directs an empire that rips tens of tons of coal a day from the Indian lands of the Navajo and Hopi. He collects figurines of bald eagles. He has built the second largest nuclear power plant in the world, Palo Verde just west of Phoenix, at a cost of $9 billion. He speaks with a large Hopi kachina peering over his shoulder from his office bookcase.

He is the native son, raised in nearby Mesa, and now he is money, power, and contentment. Once a month he flies to Washington, D.C., to check up on the Arizona congressional delegation. Candidates for office make it a point to call on him. He is conservative, Republican, and wears red neckties.

I ask him about his collection of eagles, all those little porcelain and brass objects. He offers that bewitching smile and says he doesn't know quite how it got started but it did and now everybody gives them to him. Yes, he likes eagles.

He has never really seen one in the wild. Oh, once you know, someone said look up there, an eagle!, but he couldn't really tell. It was just a big bird.

I ask him what his favorite place is in Arizona.

On the weekends he sometimes goes to his second home up in Flagstaff, more than a mile high in the pine country. He plays golf there. But his favorite place? What do I mean?

I let the question drop.

He would rather talk about Phoenix, currently the ninth largest city in the United States and a miracle of the desert, a target in the Sunbelt for real estate developers and power company executives. He wants Phoenix to be a great city and he is determined it will be. The Great City of the Southwest.

I point out that Phoenix cannot grow forever, that the place can't hold say fifteen million people.

He looks at me curiously and asks, "Why not?"

He wants to buy a ballet company, buy an opera company, buy whatever is needed. He has already helped half buy a theater company. He will make Phoenix great. He will buy. And buy.

He is a very pleasant man, a charming man. We do not talk about the desert, except of course as a reserve of raw land.

Blue

THEY PLAY A GAME here but nobody watches from a box seat. The players are called wets by those who hunt them. They cross a hot desert, a dry desert, one of North America's benchmarks for thirst and they cross with one or two gallons of water. They walk thirty, forty, fifty, sixty miles in order to score. The goal line here means not six points but a job.

Here are the rules. Get caught and you go back to Mexico. Make it across and you get a job in the fields or backrooms. Don't make it and you die.

Each month during the summer about two hundred and fifty people try the game in this particular section of western Arizona, a 3,600-square-mile stretch that runs from Yuma on the Colorado about a hundred miles eastward. Many get caught, mainly because the heat and thirst and miles grind them down. A bunch go down and wait to die.

Some die.

Nobody pays much attention to this summer sport. The players are nameless and constantly changing and so there is little identification with them or with their skills and their defeats. And the players are brown and this earns them a certain contempt and makes the attraction difficult to sell to spectators. The arena, a section of desert 100 miles long and 30 to 60 miles wide, is too unwieldy for easy viewing—no zoom shots here, no instant replay—and very uncomfortable

with its heat, dryness, serpents, and thorns. A massive folk movement is pounding its way out of Mexico and Central America and this
sector of the line and these deaths are but a small noise amid the
clamor of the American border.

Those who play this desert game do pay attention. And they learn
many things.

My education in these matters began months before. I was sitting
at my desk in September when a news story caught my eye: seven
Mexicans had died of thirst east of Yuma and several more had been
snake bitten. It seemed like a high price for a job I would not take if
offered. I began to train, walking around the city with my backpack
stuffed with five or six gallons of water. The weight and feel of the
load seemed impossible and then, before I fully appreciated this fact,
my knee went out. A month later I was in the hospital looking up at
two eyes staring over a surgical mask. The operation kept me a bit
gimpy for two months and then it was too late to pursue my idea.

By then the desert had gone cold and there was little to learn in
walking forty or fifty miles on the winter ground. I waited until June,
until the solstice of June, thinking the longest day of the year surely
would provide the heat and thirst required. The whole notion capti-
vated me. I had separated from my wife and taken a studio apartment
in a huge complex full of others in temporary flight from maimed
marriages. On the wall I taped large topographic maps of the area
where I would cross the line and march north. I sat there for hours
sipping a drink and studying the vast expanses of sand and mountain, the delicate lines tracing the Cabeza Prieta National Wildlife
Refuge, the warning announcements for the huge Air Force Gunnery range. I would move slowly northward, leave the truckstop in
Sonora where wets gather, slip through the legendary fence between
the two nations, slide across the burning ground until finally, finally,
I would come out at Interstate 8, the big road linking Phoenix and
Tucson with San Diego, come out and be safe on this artery of
commerce that followed the Gila River westward.

In the evenings I ran. In the mornings, I lifted weights. Always, I
thought about the crossing and made the journey day after day in my
mind. I told people I was angered by the news coverage of such
events, by the way the deaths were ignored or entombed in tiny
clippings. I would piously ask, "What do you think would happen if
seven people from Minnesota died out there? Why, it would be on

the network evening news!" as if such a result would make everything right again in the world. I half believed this rhetoric but it had
little to do with my desire for the crossing.

I get up at 4 A.M. and make coffee and sit in the small apartment
and stare at the maps. The women I am seeing tell me, "Don't die
out there. Don't get hurt." I smile and shrug. It is all false, all
melodrama. I do not consider getting hurt; I do not consider not
making it. That is not the threat or the attraction. I smell the aroma
of the coffee and savor the bitterness on my tongue.

I have no interest in Central America and believe it a fact of life
that the United States will meddle in the affairs of nearby countries
that are small and weak. I feel little concern about Mexicans coming
north. I don't care if they take jobs and I don't care if they are
blocked by a wall of steel and weapons and forced to live with the
nation they created, Mexico.

When I drift in my thoughts of the desert, then in those good
moments, the desert is always blue. I am going to blue desert. Of
course, this will not suffice for a newspaper so I focus on the Border
Patrol, the tactics and problems of Mexicans coming north, the
harshness of the land. But at 4 A.M. over that first cup of coffee, I
warm myself in blue desert. I have no idea why the color attracts
me. As a boy, I had a succession of hand-me-down blue suits and I
hated them and have hated the color in clothing ever since. But I
keep seeing this image and everything is blue and a great calm settles
over me.

It is late at night and we are drinking wine in a club. The woman
says, "Don't you die out there on me. You come back."

I smile and shrug and hardly hear.

Everything is blue, luminously blue.

But of course there is a difference between my imaginings over
morning coffee and the desert on a June night. The snake rattles by
my boot at 2 A.M. and then moves off a foot into a brittle bush. The
green-and-tan-banded body is only about twelve inches long. We
throw down our packs. Bill Broyles, my companion on this hike,
slowly assembles the flash unit on his camera and then pokes the
rattler to force a better display.

This is the moment I have been dreading and the key reason I
could not face the walk alone. I have this nightmare of being bitten.
It is very dark and I am alone and thirty or forty miles from roads,

doctors, and salvation. I go slowly berserk or perhaps I quickly die. The snake in my dream has an awful grin, a scaly Satan with fangs buried deep in the muscle of my calf. I can feel my flesh pulse as the reptile injects the poison into my blood.

So I have not come alone. In my backpack, I have a rope. Somewhere in the back of my head, I have this idea that if one of us is bitten, the other can tie up the victim to prevent him from wandering off into the desert in delirium, and then the lucky one will walk out for help. That is how deep run my fears and fantasies of snakebite.

Now the moment has arrived, just an instant ago I felt the snake quiver under my boot and then the rattle and then nothing at all. The small reptile simply slithered off a foot, as shocked at our meeting as I was. And I hardly moved.

As Bill works his camera I lie down on the ground four or five feet away from the snake and take a ten-minute nap. I am not afraid and I am not brave. I am absolutely indifferent.

We are twenty-odd miles into the passage. Around us are all the places I studied on the wall maps back at the apartment. If you have enough water, the names have a picturesque ring. If you do not have enough water, they sound like the lid opening on a crypt. The Lechuguilla Desert is at our backs, the Tule Desert sprawls to the south, and the dunes of the Mohawk Valley yawn before us with the sands glowing under a full moon. We are stopped on the east flank of the Copper Mountains, just north of the Cabeza Prietas. Behind us, Big Pass opens with jaws seven miles wide. Fifteen miles to the southeast, the Tinajas Altas look near enough to touch. All these places are creosote, bare ground, dry washes, stunted trees. This earth is too dry for the deer, too dry for the javelina. This is the furnace room of the Sonoran Desert.

I cannot get the map out of my head with its names, tidy brown contour lines, blue strands hinting at drainages and babble of Spanish words and prospector lingo, all struggling to nail down the land. On my faithful map, this country appears as tidy and organized as a city park.

The photo session winds down, the thirty-pound packs are shouldered and we move on. We do not talk much about the snake or about our reactions. We do not talk about thirst, hunger, or fatigue.

There is no need. I sense we are starting to lose it and I do not even consider talking about this at all.

Of course, I suppose there are good tactical reasons for not launching a discussion on the fact that we have just treated a rattlesnake as an amusing toy and a media event. But I don't think like a line commander and my silence has nothing to do with careful judgment. We do not talk because there is no need or appetite for words. We have come at least twenty miles tonight and we have more than twenty to go before the sun takes the land back.

We are two specks on an ill-defined strand of migrant trails, faint footpaths that start at truckstops just over the line in Mexico and then lance north thirty to sixty miles, depending on the angle chosen, to Interstate 8. Yuma is more than forty miles to the west and Ajo eighty to the east and in between there is not much at all. There are no springs or streams and no one lives here, no one. A few rock holes hold puddles for desert bighorns for weeks or months at a time and the rains average three inches a year and sometimes forget to come for years at a time. In the summer, say from Memorial Day to mid-September, daytime temperatures scamper right past 100 and sometimes touch 120, 125 degrees or more.

This is the basic desert of folklore, one uncluttered with annoying twentieth-century rest areas, water fountains, trail signs, and short-cuts. For me, this is clearly part of the draw. I don't have to think much here because everything is stated very plainly. I have found a place that skips the big words.

We do not know how many are out here with us this night. Before we left El Saguaro truckstop in Mexico hours ago, we watched men glide off in twos and threes and head north. But there are other spots for departure and many more are walking this desert. We are all heading for towns and points along the Interstate, places like Well-ton, Tacna, or a roadside rest area at Mohawk Pass. Little dots of flesh inching north and probably by now all hurting.

We go up against seven border patrolmen who work days, the random war games of the gunnery range and full-time companions like hunger and thirst and heat.

Score-keeping is a bit haphazard. The Border Patrol body count runs anywhere from two to twelve dead a summer but no one pretends to find all the bodies or have any real sense of how many rot undiscovered. There is a range here littered with bones and the desire to recover them is slight since a pauper burial costs the county $400. Over the past decade, I calculate at least 200 people have died on this stretch.

Jim Clarida, a Border Patrol agent at the Tacna station, tried to explain the power of the heat to me one day in late May. The afternoon before the thermometer had slapped 125 in the Tacna shade. Clarida patiently sipped his coffee, lit a smoke, and said, "Let me tell you about my son's pet rabbit."

The kid, he sighed, had raised this buck for a 4-H project and then you know how it goes. The rabbit became part of the family and stayed on. The animal lived in a cool hutch under thick vines.

Well, yesterday, he continued, the rabbit got out and ran about fifty yards before the boy caught him and put him back in the hutch. Twenty minutes later, Clarida went out and checked on him and the buck was thrashing around and heaving. Then he just died.

Clarida paused in his tale and snapped his fingers, pop! He died just like that, he smiled.

Of course Mexicans are not rabbits. Once, they found a dead man and the desert all around him was ripped up like he had gone berserk. They could see the marks on the ground where he had crawled on his belly swimming across the sand, acting as if the hot ground were a cooling sea.

Then there are those found with their shoes and clothes piled neatly beside them. Such men reach a point and decide the game is over and try to lie down and peacefully die. This is not an easy thing to do. When the cold takes a man, it is said to be like drifting off to sleep and not unpleasant. I have a friend who was drunk and womanless and depressed in a small pub in the Canadian bush. He walked out in the January night and hobbled off a mile into the snow. And then he lay down and began to fall into dreams. Calm and content, he waited for death. He eventually changed his mind and struggled out but he told me the brief taste of the grave was not bad, not bad at all.

With heat and thirst, death shows a different hand. The body temperature soars and the brain seems to cook. The flesh feels electric with pain as each cell screams out its complaint. People in such circumstances tear off their clothes in the hope of being cooled. They bury their heads in the sand in the hope of comforting their sizzling craniums. Sometimes the Border Patrol finds corpses with the mouths stuffed with sand.

Strange thoughts and desires can be unleashed. A few years ago south of Ajo, a group of Salvadoran men and women crumpled under the heat and began to die. One man, staring at a death that seemed minutes away, tried to fuck a corpse only to find that he was too far gone for even this last pleasure. Dying in the snow and cold is better. On this everyone agrees.

But still they keep coming, day after day, night after night. Some will move only during daylight because they fear the snakes. Some refuse to wear hats. Almost all carry no more than a gallon of water. The desert south of Tacna and Wellton is probably the hardest sector of the American border to cross and survive. But they keep coming and I cannot help but wonder what kind of experiences produce people willing to take on such ground.

Almost always this particular chunk of the Republic is ignored. The 125-mile drive along Interstate 8 from Gila Bend to Yuma is universally decried as a vast boredom of sand, creosote flats, vicious-looking rock piles of mountains, frightening heat, and no decent restaurants to tease the traveler. Because the land south of the highway is locked up by the military and the U.S. Fish and Wildlife Service, it is little known. There are no paved roads there, no picnic benches, no suggested scenic overlooks.

The statistics kept by the game rangers contend that 3,000 Americans a year peek into this country but the numbers are a bureaucratic fraud based mainly on those who drive a short loop road right next to Ajo. In a typical summer, maybe two or three Americans legally take out a permit and go into the hot country. And perhaps a thousand Latins who have other concerns than permits.

I was once having dinner with a woman who proceeded to tell me what a hideous drive it was to go to Yuma, to stare hour after hour at this God-forsaken wasteland. I lost my temper and told her she was a fool and she looked at me with disbelief. But I knew what she said rang with truth, that for almost everyone this country is a flat, dry tedium, something flaming past the window as the air conditioner purrs, the stereo sings, the cold beer sweats in the hand. It is not an idea or felt thing. No one sings its praises or spins legends from its emptiness. It is nowhere.

Now Bill and I are deep into this nowhere and by 2 A.M. we are facing our hurts. Our shoulders ache, our backs ache, our legs ache, and our feet ache. We drink constantly and nibble candy bars and yet our thirst never seems to end and our energy continues to decline. And we are maybe halfway.

The hunger is a fine thing. A month earlier I made a sixteen-mile night march out of this same desert with a half gallon of water and no food. The black sky flashed and sparkled with aircraft playing war and the air hung like a sweet drug full of carnal sensations. When I finally staggered into Tacna, the town's cafes were closed and I banged loudly on the kitchen door of one until a woman appeared and heard my plea. She sold me a small bag of M&Ms.

I tore the packet open and the little candies spilled out onto the gravel. I dove down to my knees and grabbed greedily at them in the dirt. She stood there towering over me and said nothing and I did not give her a moment's thought.

That kind of totally absorbing hunger is the basic menu here. It insists on your attention and yet is strangely sensuous like the feel of your hand caressing a woman's breast. It is not to be ignored.

Besides the aches and the thirst and the hunger, Bill and I sense something else, something we refuse to discuss. Our behavior with the snake had a certain flair but does not seem terribly sensible. Why did he hunker down a foot or so from the snake and keep poking at it with a stick while he fiddled with his camera? Why did I sprawl out next to the snake and nap like I was sharing a bed with a domestic cat back home?

Something is happening at a deep level in our bodies, a revolt in the cells, a shift in the chemical juices, in the intricate synapses that fire information through our flesh and that organize our muscle into motion and purpose. Our will is dissolving as our tissue loses tiny trace elements, things with names I do not even know.

We skip the snake business, brush it off as a detail, and consider the containers of water straining our shoulders. Do we really need that much water? Maybe we should pour some of it out, cut the load?

Then we stop talking about the water and march on. We do not trust our minds any longer. They seem fine and even more interesting than is usually the case but there is something different now about the way thoughts come and go. And we do not want to speak of this feeling of unreliability. How can we even trust our perceptions of warning?

I drift back to our start yesterday afternoon. In that beginning there is warmth, confidence, and good spirits. We sprawl in the shade at El Saguaro truckstop, a dot along the Mexican highway between Sonoyta, eighty miles to the east, and San Luis forty miles to the west. A man, a woman, and a baby rest on pads under a flatbed truck and wait out the afternoon heat. The man is about thirty and he stretches out and smokes. His woman nuzzles against him. The baby gurgles and plays with the man's finger.

It is 105 degrees in the shade and rising.

The truck bears Sinaloa plates, a Mexican state 600 miles south and I imagine them homeward bound. El Saguaro has no electricity, no cooling, no well. A few miles to the east is La Joya truckstop, another place of dreams. There electric lights hang from the ceiling, a television is mounted in a corner, and at La Joya also there is no electricity, no cooling, no well. Once I was there and I saw a dog eating a dead dog. The food in the cafe is simple but filling.

These two spots are the principal launching pads for the walks of *los mojados* northward. Water is sold to these travelers at about a buck and a half a gallon. At times Mexico can seem a little weak on compassion. A friend once asked an old patrón of San Luis what people did there for a livelihood.

"They eat each other's bones," he smiled.

All my many Mexicos appear at El Saguaro. There are the tall Sonorans, fairer skinned than many of their countrymen and larger because they possess less Indian blood. *Ricos,* the richer members of the Mexican economy, pull in from time to time in new cars, windows rolled up to announce they have air conditioning. They buy a bottle of pop and a bag of chips, gaze at the slumbering throng with disgust, and then depart. The truckers and poorer folk from farther down are darker and shorter and look out on the desert heat with caution written across their eyes. Forty years ago this stretch of road was sand and many died when their machines bogged down and no help came. For years some residents of San Luis and Sonoyta made a tidy little income salvaging the abandoned cars and trucks. Once a man found the skeleton of an infant on a back seat.

The Mexican poverty that always catches my eye when I am deep into the country is here launching a war of liberation. The truckstops hold small groups of men, each man carrying a clear plastic, gallon milk container full of water and a bag or knapsack with a few cans of chiles for the hike north. I once hitched a ride on this road with a Mexican in an old wreck—we had to stop twice to pour in transmission fluid—and suddenly he pointed north to men going through the fence and laughed, *"Mojados!"* Then he asked, "How good really are wages in the states?"

I lie on a cement slab and stuff down potato chips and Cokes. My body is full of apprehension. Semi drivers carefully string hammocks under their parked rigs and then climb in and sleep. Others sit in a small patio eating and drinking beer.

The baby starts crying and the man gets up, walks into the restaurant, and returns with a canteen of water. He sprinkles drops over the child's body and is very gentle. The crying stops. The woman sleeps on.

The landscape around the truckstop is almost empty of vegetation—some creosote, a few ironwoods huddling in a dry wash, but mainly rock and pale earth and glare. Behind us a road leads to a hilltop micro-wave station. We sit without electricity while high tech sings above our heads.

The Mexicans who travel this road fear the desert and fear the heat. I have walked out of this terrain and had them offer me free meals as if I were some wonder boy of the sands. Once Bill hitched a ride with a trucker on this stretch. When he asked the trucker to stop so he could hike off into the desert, the man refused.

He said, "If I let you go, you will die."

El Saguaro attracts people willing to give it a shot. Around 12:30 two men start north. They wear caps and each carries his gallon of water. Three hours later, some men get off a flatbed truck that has stopped. They carefully fold up the tarp for the driver as payment for the ride. Each of these men also has a one-gallon milk container and heads north. They wear no hats; their shirts do not cover their arms and are dark colors. For shoes, they favor sneakers.

Bill and I watch them depart into the heat. The Border Patrol has found that the men who die are usually in their twenties and quite strong. They do not fear the desert or the sun. They walk right through the heat of the day. And they die. We are both on the edge of forty. We wait.

I content myself with watching the people who must live with heat. They are drinking beer, sleeping in hammocks under trucks, sprinkling water on squawling babies.

Our preparations do not seem to be much as the hot hours roll past. We have run, lifted those weights, studied our safe little maps. Bill is basically a piece of iron, the survivor of thirteen marathons and a man who has run Pike's Peak four times. One room of his house is nothing but weights, the walls plastered with little admonitions to lift harder.

Our packs tip the scales at a little over thirty pounds and hold three gallons of water, some raisins, nuts and candy bars, extra socks, medicine, swatches of material for plastering blisters, flashlights, trousers and long-sleeved shirts, a sheet to stretch out for shade. Also, we have buried water along the route just in case we need it or run into someone else who does.

We wear hats, running shorts, t-shirts, and light boots.

Of course, there are some black spots in the training record. I sat up half the night before, drinking and drinking and could hardly sleep at all what with the phantoms stalking my dreams.

The Mexicans train differently. They arrive after long truck rides and hitchhikes and carry their one gallon of water and little or no food. They wear shabby shoes or sandals, skip hats as often as not and sometimes are decked out in black from head to foot. According to the Border Patrol, about sixty percent have made the passage before and presumably know what they are getting into. The other forty percent are virgins.

The first-timers are often dropped here by coyotes, the border's smugglers of humans, and are told that the border is a few miles away and they will meet them on the other side. The other forty or fifty miles of the route is apparently considered a detail by these smugglers. The people ignorant of the area tend to come from the interior, from jungles full of parrots or Sierras full of pines. They amble off into the hard desert and discover a different kind of world.

I watch them disappear one by one into the beginning of their education. The walls of the cafe are red and yellow, and a battery-powered radio blares, "Hotel California."

Men are busy working on the truckstop trying to install an air cooler. They fire up a tiny Honda generator to test it. The boss paddles over, a stout man in his fifties. He is dressed very nicely and makes conversation with us.

He explains that his lease on the place expires in fifteen days and he is making improvements in the hope that the landlord will renew it. He points to big holes in the roof and sighs. Out back are two privies, and he dismisses them with a sweep of the hand. He confides that he refuses to use them.

The cooler is really his grand gesture. Surely, he feels, this will win his landlord to his side.

I am charmed by this Mexican Mr. Fix-it, but a little alarm rings in the back of my head. He moves with the unmistakable air of a Mexican official, a kind of predator seldom seen in the states outside the turf of the Chicago police force.

Suddenly, he demands, "Who are you and what are you doing here?"

He produces a badge and says he is an immigration official at San Luis.

He continues his questions with "Where is your car?"

Bill tells him that we are on foot, that we love this beautiful desert and wish to hike it.

The man brushes past such nonsense and asks, "Why are you taking pictures?"

"Oh," Bill smiles, "I take them for memories, Señor."

The official gazes with interest at our bulging backpacks and visions of loot, scams, busts, and bribes dance across his features. It would be difficult to exaggerate the roguery of a Mexican official. I know a man with a federal job in one border community who regularly drives up to Arizona and buys big appliances that are barred by Mexican law from importation into the country. Once, he was heading back with a load of micro-wave ovens when a friend asked him how he proposed to get them past the Mexican customs officials. Ah, he exclaimed, but they are for the wives of the customs officials.

The man with the badge continues to wait for our reply. Bill has brought an ice axe to use as a camera tripod and the agent's eyes light up when he notices it.

"Oh," he muses, "you are prospectors, no?"

He begins to babble of lost gold mines said to be in the area and the thought of ore brings pleasure to his face. Is that not why we have come?

We smile and laugh and shrug. He will not be dissuaded. He has seen the axe.

He punctures this moment of good cheer by noting, "I could ask for your papers right now, you know. I have the right."

This is kind of a sore point for me. The night before I could not find my birth certificate or voter registration card and in any event, I resent the paperwork demanded by governments that claim to own the desert. So I have entered the Republic of Mexico illegally and I start calculating just how much money this technical error will cost me.

We smile at the man.

Then someone calls him from inside the cafe, something about the new air cooler being installed. He nods and excuses himself from us for a moment.

We grab our packs and melt into the desert to the north knowing he will never follow us into such a country.

It is 5:30 P.M. when we step off and there will be some light for three hours. The border waits five or six miles ahead and many trails streak northward to the line. We follow tracks of tennis shoes, running shoes, soccer shoes, *huaraches*, and boots. The way is lined with empty cans of fish, nectarine juice, and chiles. Black ash marks where fires fought back the night.

The trails braid and wander and cross each other, a kind of stuttered beginning to a long walk. We move along the stone walls of the Tinajas Altas mountains, walking fast, eager to leave the Mexican immigration official behind and powered like all travelers on this path by the pull of the El Dorado to the north.

Then a white masonry obelisk spikes upward a couple of hundred yards to the east. A bunch of stones on the ground at our feet spell out MEXICO/USA, and nearby a huge wooden sign stands there with its surface weathered and perfectly blank. Another and smaller sign warns that motor vehicles are forbidden.

This is the fabled border. There is no fence, just this boast of an imaginary line and footprints, everywhere footprints, and all heading one direction.

We move through the low hills, a gentle roll of land, and after a half hour, the view opens up and we can see across the Lechuguilla to Big Pass. Beyond Big Pass, puffs of smoke rise from fields being burned off near Tacna. Everything looks close enough to touch. It seems impossible that the hike will take more than two, maybe even three hours. The light weakens from white to gold, the valley shines with perfectly spaced creosote and is lanced down the center by ironwood and palo verde lining Coyote Wash. We hardly speak now. The rhythm of our footsteps constitutes our language and to a degree, we are struck dumb by the order and hugeness of the landscape. The big valley could serve as the garden of a Zen monastery.

Two and a half hours out of El Saguaro truckstop, we reach a fork in the trail that leads off to Tinajas Altas, a series of nine rock tanks. All human footprints arc away from the water. All coyote tracks race left toward the water. The small pools lie hidden from view on the steep rock side of the mountain. The rains fill them and historically they have been the only sure water between Agua Dulce spring sixty miles to the east, and Yuma, forty miles to the west. Once hundreds of graves were visible around the tanks and the path was lined on both sides with the mummified carcasses of upright horses and mules. The federal boundary survey of the 1890s found a prospector dead just below the first tank. His fingers were worn raw from trying to climb the rock. He had been too weak to make it to water and died a few yards from his salvation.

At this place, a key medical paper on thirst was created in 1905. W. J. McGee, a nationally known scientist and renowned desert rat, was camped here in August while cancer ate at his body. Pablo Valencia dropped in.

Valencia had been lost for six-and-a-half days and for five days he had lived by drinking his urine. His bowels had completely shut down during this experience and for two days his kidneys failed. He had undergone a change in what we moderns might call his values. He threw all his money away; he hallucinated a desert saturated with wet sand. He had dreams of dying and he had days of staying on the march. He made it to Tinajas Altas and was saved. McGee had heard this bellowing, this deep roaring, a sound he likened to a bull, and wandered out and found the man.

When Bill almost died because coyotes dug up his water supply, he was retracing Valencia's wanderings.

We pass Tinajas Altas without stopping and strike out across the desert for Big Pass, following the footprints of Mexicans. A little after 8 P.M. we stop and eat and drink. We have been drinking steadily, making no effort to conserve water. The problem is not running out of water but pouring it into our bodies fast enough. We sweat like beasts but we can only drink like human beings.

Bill checks his feet for blisters, the sun sinks, and the light goes from gold to rose to gone. We sit beside an ancient trail etched on a field of stone. Broken pottery fragments lie about. I smile and think of an Indian tripping, and I imagine strange curses in the air as the clay vessel smashes on the ground. The Lechuguilla wears the marks of many journeys. Aboriginal trails cross car tracks, tank tracks, game tracks, Mexican tracks, our tracks. Pieces of spent military hardware litter the ground. I can see traces in the sand of lizards, rats, and sidewinders.

Big Pass is so near, so very near. We joke that this walk may be too easy, that Big Pass will be ours in an hour or so. But from Tinajas Altas to the Big Pass is 13.5 miles as the raven flies. We are not ravens. We dodge clumps of creosote, fall into rat holes, stumble down into washes, detour ironwoods, watch for cactus, and zigzag across the terrain.

The moon slams the ground with white light. At our backs, Cipriano Pass knifes between the Tinajas Altas and Gila Mountains, a cut the Border Patrol calls Smuggler's Pass. It is part of a shortcut to the Interstate and the town of Wellton, a nine-hour route. The various trails whipping across the Lechuguilla all have one goal: avoid capture. The Mexicans say that they come across this pan of sand and heat because they think their chances of evading the Border Patrol are enhanced. The Border Patrol denies this and claims such hikes are foolish risks. But then, their federal commitment to the game is not as complete as the Mexicans' —the referee never has the same feel for the sport as the lineman.

We stumble across the valley. The heat ceases to matter, not because it goes away, but because we go into it and join with it and can imagine no life separate from it. The night is soft with warmth, the moon is up, and I feel my sweat as the air brushes against my flesh with a light touch. I have no desire to be cool and no desire to be elsewhere. I do not think of the Border Patrol or of snakes or of thirst, fatigue, thorns, blisters, hunger, and pain.

I think of my wife. I look at the moon and think she is looking up at that moon and we are together. This lunar unity strikes me suddenly as a great insight. The soil crunches under my feet and my legs bleed from the small tears of thorns. I look at that moon.

The collapse of my marriage has not been tidy. I left; then there were no words. Then there were talks. She has seen a counselor and this, she tells me, has helped.

I am sitting in the living room, an exhibition hall of her taste and the sofa is soft and comfortable. My body is rigid, the muscles hard with tension. She speaks and the words pour out for more than an hour—angry jabs, blunt charges, an inventory of my sins. I do not disagree. I listen and I am mute. This is all necessary. The words must be said. She weeps.

We make love on the floor.

Then it falls apart again. The pattern repeats. We begin the process of divorce. Then we have dinner and laugh. I bury myself in work; I go through the motions of preparing for the long walk; I drink.

She has large breasts hanging from a thin body. She finds a lump. There are many tests and the results give different answers. I can see a blue vein just below the surface on one breast, a faint pulsing river of blood. There are more tests. After weeks, they decide: cancer. The breast must be cut off.

She tries to be brave but after a while this ceases to be enough. She asks me if I can imagine what this means, if I can conceive of mutilating my sexual identity. Of course, I cannot.

The water sloshes in my pack, my feet pound along like a metronome on a grand piano, and I look up at that moon. In three days, she will be wheeled into surgery. I have had her schedule the operation so that it will not interfere with my walk, with this story. I am inflexible on this point and cannot be budged. My work has become my religion and I use it to keep at bay all demands and duties. She looks into my eyes and sees a sullen stranger there.

They will cut off the breast and they will search her tissue to see—to see if more must be hacked off her body. She stares at a fear much larger than Big Pass. She wants to make love all the time. The shambles of our marriage does not matter. She is like a gladiator about to go into the arena and she wants it all while there is still time.

She has never been more alive and her senses grow keen with this fact of cancer. "Can you imagine what this means to me?" she says. I hear her voice cutting across the Lechuguilla. She collects toys and stuffed animals; she collects images of pigs; she worships cats. As children we both happened to read the same edition of Hans Christian Andersen, one with intricate and magical plates by Nathaniel Wyeth. The illustrations promised a world far beyond my reach.

"Can you imagine?" she asks.

I enter a serenity of walking, dodging cactus, and always those thorns on the small shrubs and large trees slice my arms and legs. I walk into the limbs, these I do not detour and I take pleasure in crashing ahead, in the sound of thorns raking across my nylon pack.

The moon—I draw power from the moon. I think—no, I do not think, I know with certainty—that I will make it and she will make it and that we are both looking at the moon and I will pull her through the dark cave of anesthesia and the knife and the pain and the huge bandage wrapped across where her breast once spread as a generous mound. My will becomes like iron and I know. I am a tiny dab of flesh dragging across a huge valley in the moonlight but I am larger than the mountains, stronger than hard metals, because I know. I know. I feel no guilt now.

Everywhere the earth is beauty. The mountains lift sharply off the valley floor, rockpiles almost naked of plants. Beauty. The moon flashes off the stone walls. Beauty. The creosote, the much derided greasewood, stands spaced like a formal garden. Beauty. Stars crowd the sky and I can hear them buzzing with the fires of their explosive gases. I tear the wrapper from a Granola bar and crunch the grains between my teeth. I tip the plastic jug up to my lips and swallow. I lock on the moon. Beauty.

The desert tonight is an enormous theater full of tracks made by men and women and sometimes children inching north. The air is empty of sound. We all struggle toward Big Pass alone and this is necessary. We are always alone, everywhere alone, but here this fact cannot be denied. It is a condition of this place and other people cannot, this time, alter or obscure that insight.

A flare bursts over our heads. The military sharpens itself for war. We enter a cleared strip of ground, a target area. Something finned like a bomb fragment squats on the sand. And then everything turns blue. The mountains rise azure, the ocotillo waves blue wands, the creosote whispers by my feet, and everything is awash with a rich, bright blue. At first the color is ahead and then I enter it like water and the blue is everywhere. It does not coat the surface but seems to come from the center of things. I look at my hand and the skin glows with blue pigment.

I do not hesitate or wonder. I do not speculate that the sugar flow to my brain has declined, that the pangs of dehydration have addled my mind, that some vast chemical change in my body is altering my perceptions. I have entered this blue world and I accept it totally. It means peace. I long to see a coyote cutting across the flats on a night hunt, to see a blue coyote and hear a blue yell under a blue moon. My senses quicken and yet dull. The peace works deep into my muscle and my body works harder and harder and yet feels ease. I begin to glide. Ahead Big Pass waits with dark blue jaws.

I glance at Bill ten yards off to my side and lurching as I must be over the uneven surface mined with holes, plants, and bad footing. But I glide. I know I glide.

Blue.

Other travelers have probably tasted a different, less serene Lechuguilla. In 1976, the Border Patrol found men harnessed to a cart equipped with auto tires for wheels. They were hauling it across this very desert where Bill and I now stumble. They were on no road or trail. The cart was full of marijuana.

Once Bill was walking a few miles to the south and discovered tracks made by wheels. He carefully measured the marks and realized they were made by wagons in the nineteenth century. I have a friend who served in this area during World War II. He says there is a wagon train lying in ruins in the sands, a relict of a party massacred by bandits a century ago. Men training for the war sighted the wreck. No one has seen it since.

There is a mass grave near a big tree according to old accounts, a burying place for a man, a woman, and their children. The horse died, the wagon stopped, the family perished within ten miles of the waters of Tinajas Altas. People report visiting the site from time to time. Bill and I have tried to find it. There are so few large trees in the Lechuguilla, the task should be simple. We always fail.

To the north and west a ways, the military prepares to test a silo for the MX missile system. Giant doors will endure huge blasts to determine if this clever shell game with the Soviets will really work. Someday, future wanderers can search for this site.

Thoughts trip across my mind without obvious logic. They are soft, soggy clumps of feeling. They produce no argument or insight but seem like the pulps of fruit lying together in a bowl. I solve nothing and do not desire solutions. We are on a treadmill toward Big Pass. The rock walls glow under the fat moon.

Steps. Step after step after step. We tire, we stop. We time the break with our digital watches. Five minutes and no more. We must move, move, move. Move dammit, MOVE.

We must make Big Pass.

We do not ask why.

We do not speak at all.

About 12:30 A.M., Big Pass finally swallows us. We have drunk less than one gallon of water apiece. We are thirsty, constantly thirsty but we cannot seem to pour the fluid into our bodies any faster. My legs are tired, my shoulders sore, and I am beginning to feel the bones in my feet. We move on.

The tracks we lost at Tinajas Altas now reappear and I smile at the reunion. The soccer shoe is back. The running shoe also. We have all converged at the Pass and just beyond the gap, we all take a dirt road hugging against the Copper Mountains. Now the hunt begins in earnest.

The Border Patrol knows tracks. They can read prints on foot, from trucks and from aircraft. Once they pick up a fresh trail below the Interstate, they stay with it until the footprints tell them that the people have gotten out. In part this is because once the tracks make it to the freeway, the person is likely to hitch a ride and slip beyond the federal reach. And in part, this is because if the tracks do not make it to the Interstate, then the person is still in the desert and to the Border Patrol this means the person could be dying. Jim Clarida, the man who watched his son's rabbit die from the heat, once tracked a man for seventy-five miles.

The Mexicans in turn do their very best to avoid the trackers. They walk backwards to confuse their pursuers. They drag brush to obliterate their footprints. They often stay off the roads. When caught, they ask the agents how they bagged them. The agents tell them. The game demands certain courtesies.

After Big Pass, the drag roads begin. The Border Patrol pulls old tires on chains to wipe the dirt clean. Then they know any tracks are fresh. The drag roads are checked often, on the ground and from the air. When a new sign is spotted, the hunt begins.

Tonight, no one seems interested in hiding their tracks. The road shows clear sign. It is now 1 A.M. and the Border Patrol shift will not begin until 6 A.M. Perhaps, everyone counts on being past the Interstate by then. Or perhaps everyone is too weary to care.

The game is played seriously but without anger. If a Mexican cannot make it, his companions often go to the Border Patrol and turn themselves in so that help can be sent to the person left behind. The Border Patrol responds. If someone is trapped in the desert, they say he is down. And that is serious business.

The agents seldom face resistance. Some of the Mexicans have been caught many times in this sector. It is a game. Once Clarida cornered a man in the brush. Suddenly the man walked out and gave himself up. Clarida recognized him as someone he had once rescued. "Anyone else I would have run from," he said, "but I owe you this one."

By 2 A.M. I feel ruin in my limbs. It is not a question of being strong or fit. Such things no longer matter. Something is happening to my body and I cannot alter this decline. The rattlesnake briefly buzzes beneath my foot, the photo is taken, the incident filed but not discussed. We can now see the Interstate more than twenty miles ahead, a thin strand of lights beckoning.

A couple of years back, a nineteen-year-old came out and said his uncle and father were down. They had no water; the father had been snakebitten. The Border Patrol found them a few days later working on a ranch along the Gila River. The father and uncle had walked through their thirst and had drunk their urine. They had poulticed the snakebite with the flesh of a cactus.

The father was sixty years old. He was very angry that his son had gone to the Border Patrol.

We gaze ahead at Tacna, at the big road, at Mohawk Pass, at the twinkling lights of other people and the promise of shade, water, food, rest. We have twenty miles more.

We have entered the killing ground.

The people who come this way do not die in the heart of the desert; they go down near their goals. They go down because there is nothing left in them, not even a tiny spark to propel them one more mile.

We begin to consider dumping our water at a point up ahead. When we reach the mouth of a certain canyon. We will be only twelve miles from Tacna. Then, the water must go. Surely nothing can stop us from covering only twelve miles and to be free of the weight of the water would be an utter joy. Why, to keep carrying all this water is madness. We are sure of this fact. Dammit, we will get rid of the stuff. We are not fools. We will pour it out.

The calves in my legs tighten, the bones in my feet hurt, the hips grind and grow sore with each stride. My pack cuts into my shoulders and food no longer seems to work. I eat and walk a ways and the energy disappears. I drink but need more water. I envision drilling straight into my belly, auguring a big hole and just pouring the water in. I will use a funnel and not spill a drop.

The night is still a blue dream. The desert can never be better than what greets my eyes. The forms cannot be questioned. The night world brings no fears. Bats fly just over our heads and they are friends. I am certain of this. An owl lifts off a saguaro and I stop and stare with worship. Nighthawks sweep just off the ground.

Across the blue valley, the Mohawks glow. Once a woman lost all hope on the flanks of the Mohawks. She was just a few short miles from the Interstate and the roadside rest there with its ramadas of shade, its bathrooms, its tap water. She ripped her clothes off, article by article and walked up a canyon and then scaled the rock slope. From up there she could see everything and it must have looked so lovely to her, seeing the green fields, the towns, and snug houses, the traffic, the big highway, the lazy course of the river. Behind she left her dress, her shoes, her panties, her bra littered along her trail.

They never found her body.

The night, the delicious night, denies such stories. The night insists on beauty.

But we hurt. Our bodies whisper: Yes, the stories are here.

At 4 A.M., we strike another drag road, wide and clean and hungry for our footprints. The moon is down and our pace is two miles an hour. We drift closer to the Coppers where we have cached water, all part of our grand strategy. Six gallons lie buried under the sand. We do not touch them and are amused by their uselessness. The water mocks our thirst. We possess this treasure but we cannot get it into our bodies.

We fall down on the road and eat and drink and watch a red glow grow in the east. We empty our packs of canteens and keep only a gallon. The rest we set out for whoever needs it, whoever comes after us. The brotherhood.

Originally, we thought we might stop at dawn in this area, wait out the murderous heat of the day and finish the following evening. We reject this idea now. We want out; that is part of it. But also we want to beat the Border Patrol. We want to win, to gain the big road before they can catch us. We have been playing the game too hard to be indifferent to the final score.

I walk off a ways into the desert, squat down, and take a shit. The sun comes on stronger. The literature of hiking is almost devoid of the simple pleasure of pissing and shitting at will. It is replete with tips on how to dispose of wastes, how to protect babbling brooks from pollution, how to leave a clean camp. But nothing on this pleasure, this return to infancy when there is no distance between the desire and the act.

I feel like I can walk no farther. I feel like I can walk forever. My body, my tired, sore body, is simply something I drag along and I cannot imagine the trip ever ending.

The traffic on the Interstate can now be seen clearly, trucks storming toward Los Angeles markets, cars cruising with the air conditioning blowing hard. I hear the rumble of the engines and delight in the sound of machines.

Bill and I get up and trudge on. We must go twelve miles. We must. We cannot beat the dawn, but we will fight the sun; we will war against the rays. We refuse to stop. Every hour, we pause briefly, drink, snack, and lie down. Then we stagger up, our legs stiff as boards. Tacna seems just ahead but hour by hour comes no nearer. We dream of Tacna, a hamlet of 100 people. Bill sees iced tea, and ice cream; he makes out a waitress holding up a cone and beckoning. We shuffle more than walk, our feet scraping across the soil.

The sun comes up with unbelievable force. I shudder under the rays like a vampire caught far from my coffin. All around us are the unmarked spots where the last dramas of the dying take place. One man went down a mile south of the Interstate. He set fire to a tree in hopes that the smoke would bring help. They found his body.

The dying can be very quick. A few weeks before a man left El Saguaro truckstop at 4 P.M. on a Saturday. By 9 P.M. Sunday he was in a body bag in Tacna. He was twenty-eight. Sometimes the Border Patrol finds people too far gone to risk the ride to the hospital in Yuma. They take them to a grocery in Tacna and put them in the beer cooler in hopes of lowering their body temperatures.

None of these tales stops the flow of people. There was an old man who crossed this desert with his son and nephew. The two boys died ten miles south of the Interstate. The old man was caught and shipped back to Mexico. A week later, he was caught again crossing the same desert with a girl of eighteen. So far the Border Patrol in the Tacna sector has nabbed that old man fifteen times.

We walk on. We must have walked on. But there is no memory of this. We walk on.

We reach Tacna at 9:48 A.M. We have made the crossing in sixteen hours, seventeen minutes, drunk a gallon and a half of water each, and have nothing to say. We have probably walked forty-five miles, but this figure, like our careful recording of the time elapsed, means very little. The weather has been very cool for this country, surely no more than 110.

I will write a story, the newspaper will print it, and there will be awards, the trinkets of the business. But this will happen later.

Now there are other tasks at hand. I must call Tucson and let them know we are out. I fumble at the push buttons of the pay phone and keep getting the operator of an overseas line. I persist and after forty minutes make the simple connection. I begin to grasp what has happened to me. My mind does not work in this world.

We enter a cafe and eat a breakfast and drink iced tea after iced tea. The food is flat. The cool drinks lack pleasure. We consume coffee, pop, ice cream, eggs, sausage, hash browns, beef, lamb, soup, beer. The gorging continues for hours.

I walk into a bar and order a Budweiser longneck. I cannot sit. My limbs ache too much. I recline on the floor. The bartender says nothing. The Mexicans are still out there. They were there yesterday, they are there today, and they will be there tomorrow and tomorrow and tomorrow. And they cannot walk in here. They are huddling by an irrigation ditch and drinking deeply and then walking ten more miles, fifty more miles, one hundred more miles, whatever it takes to find work. I feel the rush of energy that must be pushing such people. I hear this force pounding like a mighty heart somewhere to the south.

But mainly as I lie there, I feel it all slip away and my senses deaden under the blandishments and delights of my civilization. When I get home in a day I will write the newspaper story in four hours, a torrent of words, statistics, and suggestions on this illegal immigration problem. But I will not mention my wife. There will be nothing about the cancer, the scalpel incising the soft white flesh topped by the faint pink nipple. I will not find room for the insistent feeling that she will triumph, the conviction that everything can be overcome. I will skip my notion that we both looked up at the same moon. And I will write nothing of blue desert. Nor will I speak of that place to anyone.

I have exited the only ground where I truly trust my senses. Most of the Southwest is beyond my belief and strikes me as an outpost of American civilization with the exiled desert merely a faint, scenic mural stretching behind the powerlines and skyscrapers. But the Lechuguilla, the Tule, the Mohawk dunes, these places have a weight with me that makes the cities of my people seem light and insubstantial. There is no point in reasoning with me on this matter. When I touch the steel towers of the Sunbelt, they feel like cobwebs soon to be dispersed by an angry wind. When I touch the earth I feel the rock hard face of eternity.

But as I lie on the saloon floor I can hardly believe in the country I have just left. I feel the bubbles of the beer against my tongue and savor the sour taste. I am busy killing experience with categories and words and leads, striking at it like it were a serpent to be slain and made into a safe skin, perhaps a belt or hatband.

And then I fall back again and see only one word. Blue. Always blue.

They play a game here. We play a game here.

He tells me he has been in on the kill of 249 mountain lions and is anxious to bag number 250. I have come here seeking such talk. Nathan Ellison is a great guide and a great hunter. His home, twenty-odd miles up Cherry Creek under the cliffs of the Mogollon Rim, sits perched between the last northern fingers of the Sonoran Desert and first serious claims of the big pinery to the north. He is the fourth generation of his people to relish the Tonto country of Gila County and all his people have been great hunters. It is in the blood.

This region is a refuge for wild men. One summer day in 1964 when the first motorcycle braved the dirt road into neighboring Young, Arizona, some of the boys drinking at Moon's Saloon came outside and shot the tires out. They just wanted a closer look. One of the West's great range wars bloodied nearby Pleasant Valley, a combat so efficient that it left hardly any survivors and almost no descendants in the area. The old families living in these canyons were almost all founded by horse thieves and cattle rustlers and this is not denied or a matter of shame.

Ellison sits in his living room/den surrounded by bear skins, lion skins, deer heads, elk heads, bighorn sheep heads. His home is a kind of Mecca for those still seeking the game. And he is a demon on lions. He allows that at a pass close by, he has, over the years, brought down thirty-three. The lions kill calves. The men of the Tonto kill lions. This has been going on more than a century.

He is in his fifties now, his face florid, his hands hard from work. He ranches a bit, but the family spread has been so reduced by the attrition of years and the rules of the Forest Service that it no longer provides a full living. So Ellison guides, drives a grader on the local roads, functions as the deputy sheriff in this portion of the county. His face becomes animated when he recalls a hunt—and there have been so many. Last fall he guided sportsmen to thirteen bears.

Now the land is changing ownership all around him. New money from Phoenix and elsewhere has bought up most of the ranches as tax shelters and toys. People who marry money or run furniture stores or concrete businesses or make big bucks as doctors and lawyers—all these outlanders have practically swallowed the Tonto piece by piece. Ellison and his kind are in far more jeopardy than the lions they both curse and love. They cannot conceive of a world without the big cats taking down their calves, ripping the throats of deer and elk. And the cats, year after year, seem to hold even in numbers and no amount of killing has ever been able to comb the canyons and rim rocks clean of the predators. But families like the Ellisons—they are going and going fast.

They are the old West and for a time the Sunbelt ignored them and left them huddled in the hard country and endless canyons just below the Mogollon. They were legend. Zane Gray had a cabin here and cranked out books about families still living on this ground. But the loopholes and bonuses of the Internal Revenue Service code have fallen on the Tonto and the people who like to hunt and raise some cattle are no match for the people who want to ride horses and raise up a tax shelter.

The New West takes no prisoners.

On the drive up the creek to Ellison's, I noticed a newly rehabilitated ranch house along the road. The paint was fresh and bright but the thing looked wrong. All the windows were gone and inside someone had flung big rocks through the newly plastered walls, broken to fragments the new toilets and sinks, ripped doors from hinges, defiled, it seemed, every square foot of the building.

Except for these fine wooden cabinets in the kitchen which were completely untouched.

I ask Ellison about the house and what happened there.

His face brightens again.

The ranch hand down there, he explains, fixed the house up from one end to the other as his place to live. He did everything. He was a very handy man, and even made the cabinets, which Ellison allows are real jewels. And then when he finished, the place sold to new owners, outside owners from Phoenix, he believes.

The new owners told the ranch hand he was no longer needed. And then before you knew it, the place had been vandalized. Ellison couldn't remember a single instance of anything like that happening before on Cherry Creek.

I ask him if he has any suspects, seeing how he is the deputy sheriff in this area.

He thinks, and says the whole thing is puzzling, but as near as he can figure whoever did it was furious and went from room to room just busting up everything, all the walls and windows, the hot water heater, the new appliances, everything. And then when he got almost finished he took one look at those beautiful wooden cabinets and just could not do it. Just could not destroy such workmanship.

I ask what he will do if he runs into his suspect.

He says he'll tell him he shouldn't come around Cherry Creek for a while. He should get himself a job somewhere else, maybe up on the Rim, for a year or maybe two. That's what he might do.

But those cabinets, he allows. They're really something. A man must have put his heart and soul into those cabinets, you know?

CHARLES BOWDEN was for three years a reporter for the *Tucson Citizen*, an afternoon daily newspaper. His stories covered everything from murder to copper strikes to interviews with Santa Claus and politicians. He became acquainted with the scientific floor of desert understanding and the political tumult of desert development while a researcher at the Office of Arid Lands Studies at the University of Arizona. He now lives in Tucson as a freelance writer, a pastime he describes as "practically a free ticket to the asylum." Nevertheless, he is author of *Killing the Hidden Waters* (1977, 1985), *Street Signs Chicago: Neighborhood and Other Illusions of Big-City Life* with Lewis Kreinberg (1981), and *Frog Mountain Blues* (with photographs by Jack W. Dykinga), published by the University of Arizona Press in 1987.

CPSIA information can be obtained at www.ICGtesting.com
Printed in the USA
BVOW050721090911

270880BV00001B/98/P

9 780816 510818